THE
SUPERNATURAL
POWER OF A
TRANSFORMED
MIND

ACCESS
to a LIFE
of MIRACLES

THE
SUPERNATURAL
POWER OF A
TRANSFORMED
MIND

ACCESS
to a LIFE
of MIRACLES

BY BILL JOHNSON

Destiny Image₍ᵣ₎ Publishers, Inc.
P.O. Box 310
Shippensburg, PA 17257-0310

"Speaking to the Purposes of God for This Generation
and for the Generations to Come"

ISBN 0-7684-2252-3

For Worldwide Distribution
Printed in the U.S.A.

This book and all other Destiny Image, Revival Press,
MercyPlace, Fresh Bread, Destiny Image Fiction,
and Treasure House books are available
at Christian bookstores and distributors worldwide.

18 19 20 / 15 14

For a U.S. bookstore nearest you, call **1-800-722-6774**.
For more information on foreign distributors,
call **717-532-3040**.
Or reach us on the Internet:
www.destinyimage.com

DEDICATION

I dedicate this book to my dad, M. Earl Johnson, who went home to be with Jesus in January of 2004. He was and is my hero. His dignity in life was only surpassed by his dignity in death. The integrity that he showed in his public ministry was the same integrity he displayed at home. He walked in humility in the midst of opposition, and never bowed to the fear of man. He was ultimately a worshiper. As such he valued the Presence of God more than the favor of man. Yet, he was highly favored, and rightly so. He was a true general in the army of God—and my greatest encourager.

"I love you Dad, and miss you very, very much. I am running with my spiritual inheritance, and will be faithful to your legacy."

ACKNOWLEDGEMENTS

Joel Kilpatrick — Thanks for taking my transcripts and making them worthy of print. "You are wonderful!"

Lance Wallnau — Your comments on "Desire" and "Co-laboring" made a noticeable impact, and appear in this book. Thanks.

Judy Franklin, my administrative assistant — Thanks for your great encouragement, faithful service, and wonderful advice. (Also, thanks for helping me find the right "gates.")

Special thanks to my staff — You are the most amazing group of revivalists I have ever known. Only eternity will reveal the full impact of your sacrificial lifestyle. I live in your debt.

My children, Eric & Candace, Brian & Jenn, and Gabriel & Leah — Thank you for faithfully running with your spiritual inheritance. May you truly build your floor upon my ceiling, and train my grandchildren to do the same. I love you MASSIVE!

And finally to my mom — "Dad's greatness was only equaled by your own. Thanks for demonstrating the value of family, excellence, and beauty, and insisting that I write. I love you."

ENDORSEMENTS

This book will rock your boat and set you ablaze with world-changing faith! Lethal! Dangerous in the hands of be-lieving believers—the contents of this book could start anoth-er reformation—or even greater! Shake off doubt and unbelief and take the plunge into a life of supernatural activ-ity all centered around a supernatural God!

James W. Goll
Encounters Network
Author, *The Seer, Wasted on Jesus,*
and *The Lost Art of Intercession*

Radical lovers of God hunger to experience the fullness of who He is. Bill Johnson's book, *The Supernatural Power of a Transformed Mind* leads us into a glorious participation in the divine nature. He brilliantly demonstrates that becoming co-laborers with our Beloved Lord is our divine destiny. If you long to see His kingdom come on earth as it is in heaven, Bill's book will be a powerful inspiring guide.

Heidi G. Baker, Ph.D.
Director & Founder of Iris Ministries
Co-Author, *There's Always Enough*
International Conference Speaker

"Bill—I had a chance to go over in detail your two books (*The Supernatural Power of a Transformed Mind* and *When Heaven Invades Earth*). Rare stuff that encourages me to no end. Yes, we are seriously damaged if we are not intensely, utterly set on receiving all the grace that our God has for us—and it's already paid for...

In these last days I'm setting my hope in Jesus on not being a part of the usual cycles of church history during which revival comes and then goes again. Let's never look back, and may God graciously allow us to build on all that has been poured out already. You are a key part of what He is doing in the world.

Rolland Baker, Ph.D.
Director & Founder of Iris Ministries
Co-Author, *There's Always Enough*
International Conference Speaker

Only a man who lives and moves in the presence of the God of revelation could write this book. And those who read it will find that same revelation flowing out from them into the streets and beyond—to the next generation. The reformation that Bill Johnson started with his first book is sure to be accelerated with this one. We recommend it with all our hearts.

Wesley and Stacey Campbell
Founders—Be A Hero
Producers and Authors of *Praying the Bible*

Bill's teaching presents some of the most revelatory insights I've heard. The material in this book challenges me to go higher. Kingdom mindsets are important in ministering the Kingdom of God. The Bible is clear: as a man "thinks in His heart, so is he" (Prov. 23:7). If you want to cultivate kingdom thinking and have God's Kingdom become a greater reality in your life, this new book is a must read.

Todd Bentley
Evangelist/Revivalist
Founder of Fresh Fire Ministries

Bill Johnson's *The Supernatural Power of a Transformed Mind* is key to the issue of advancing God's Kingdom on the earth. It is filled with deep personal insights from one of the leading teachers and visionaries in the church today. Equally contagious is Bill's passion to see God's will done in us as it is done in heaven. A must read for those desiring to live in the dunamis power of a transformed mind.

Larry Randolph
International Conference Speaker
Author, *User Friendly Prophecy*

Wow! This book takes us to another level. Not only does God want to have His kingdom come on earth as it is in heaven, but He wants to do it through us. Bill Johnson does a wonderful job in this second book in laying out God's plan to transform our minds in order that we will become kingdom minded to exhibit the realm of God's miraculous power into a desperate world. This book will not only deliver you but will empower you through God to deliver them.

Cal Pierce
Director, Healing Rooms Ministries
Spokane, Washington
International Conference Speaker

It has been said that a man with an experience is never at the mercy of a man with an argument. There are many who preach the present reality of the Kingdom with scriptural accuracy but remain experientially sterile. Bill Johnson's provocative perspective on the Kingdom of God will teach you to see what you believe rather than believing what you see.

Randall Worley
Headwaters Ministries

The "Spirit of Wisdom and Revelation" is upon Bill's new book, *The Supernatural Power of a Transformed Mind.* This is a must read for everyone who desires to walk in the supernatural.

Che Ahn
Senior Pastor, Harvest Rock, Pasadena, CA
Founder and President of Harvest International Ministries
Author and International Conference Speaker

Bill Johnson has once again given us a gift. With skillful use of pen and paper he takes us into a rarely visited inner world, the mind of a miracle worker. Bill has the unique ability to make the supernatural life seem so natural that unbelief in any form looks like an absurdity. This second book in his series on the supernatural abounds with gems and insights that collectively form a framework to train and renew the mind to take on the limitless possibilities of the mind of Christ. When enough people live with the mentality Bill describes, a collective tipping point will occur in one generation and the realm of healings and miracles will be as easy to access as the new birth is today.

Lance Wallnau
President of the Lance Learning Group

CONTENTS

FOREWORD

Bill Johnson is doing a follow-up of his first book, "*When Heaven Invades Earth.*" Bill's words are, "This book captures the new things I have learned in the years since the first book was written. It explores areas I had not conceived of.

Bill producing this inspirationally challenging book is in illustrious company. Saint Peter wrote two books: I and II Peter. The second book was a follow up of the first book with much more added information. Luke wrote two books. The first one was one of the four Gospels, "St. Luke's Gospel." The second book Luke authored was, "The Book of Acts." It was a continuum of the Gospel story. Paul wrote two letters to Timothy. Paul also wrote two letters to the believers in Thessalonica and two letters to the believer's in Corinth. All these letters were included in the 66 books of the Bible. In II Corinthians 1:15, Paul told them he planned on visiting them and conferring on them a "second benefit" or a "second blessing" (Berkeley Bible).

I've read the manuscript to Bill's new book and believe Bill is in the good company of Peter, Luke, and Paul who also wrote second books. Just as Paul brought a second blessing to the Corinthians, Bill Johnson's, *The Supernatural Power of a*

Transformed Mind, will give a "second" blessing to those who have read the first book.

You'll be doubly blessed reading the part on co-laboring. Chapter 10 is titled, "Dreaming with God," and chapter 11 shares, "Inheriting the Supernatural." Both chapters were informative, innovative and instructing. In areas where I had been "waiting for the Lord to move," Isaiah 30:18 reminds us that the Lord is waiting for us. Bill's book enables you to discover how to step into the stream of God's unlimited blessing and become a part of the on-going supernatural works of God.

I was able to share with Pastor Bill a Greek word found in Ephesians 4:23, "Be renewed in the spirit of your mind." The Greek word for *renewed* is ANANEOO (ann-ann-neh-oh'oh). The word for *renewed* is a compound Greek word ANA, meaning to repeat or doing over again, and NEOS which means: "youthful, young." You can interpret, "Renewed in the spirit of your mind," as "Think young."

Reading Bill Johnson's new book is spiritually invigorating and rejuvenating. Read it and you'll end up "thinking young." The very antithesis to, "stale, dry, arid, tasteless religious rhetoric." Think young!

Dick Mills
International Conference Speaker
Author, *God's Word For You* and *Marriage Bliss*

FOREWORD

Bill Johnson is a man of God who enjoys God and who is living what he writes. He is a man who has revelation into who we are in Christ and its ramifications that is definitely outside the box of traditional thinking, but not outside Scripture. His new book helps us deal with the promises of the Bible in a spiritual manner that isn't limited by the traditions and human rationalisms that have reduced God to a "god made in our image." Bill's love of the word of God is apparent in *The Supernatural Power of a Transformed Mind,* but it is equally true that Bill has a great love for the Spirit of God and for experiencing all that is promised in the Bible. There is a noticeable increase in Bill's authority and understanding of spiritual realms, especially in regard to healing over the past few years that I have known him. I love to spend time with him because of his great hunger to learn and experience more of the promises of God in his life and church.

The latter chapters of the book especially call us out into a greater experience of co-laboring with God, greater than many of us were ever taught in Bible college and seminary was possible. I couldn't help but think of the similarity between the latter chapters of his book and the recent comments of Dr.

Charles Kraft, which I believe he also states in his recent book *Confronting Powerless Christianity*. Dr. Kraft believes it is a principle of the spiritual world that both the devil and God have need of finding a person through whom they must work in agreement to accomplish their desires. Now, I know that God is sovereign, but in His sovereignty He can freely choose to work in this manner if it so pleases him. However, Bill goes even farther in his understanding of God's heart to co-labor with us. He goes beyond God looking for someone with whom to partner to carry out His will to God wanting to partner to carry out his adopted son or daughter's will or desire. Of course Bill indicates that this is only after the person has been born again and is delighting themselves in God. The implications of this principle were powerfully illustrated, especially in regard to Christian businesspeople.

This book is needed in this hour as a wake-up call to the "greater things than these shall you do" promise of Jesus. Bill's message regarding the Kingdom of God is important for the time in which we live. Jesus didn't say that he was not going to return until the "gospel" was preached in all nations, he said he wasn't going to return until the "gospel of the Kingdom" is preached to all nations. What Bill and I mean by this distinction is that for too long many have limited this promise of Jesus to preaching of forgiveness through grace while not including the other aspects of the Kingdom message, especially the aspects of healing and deliverance.

If it was true in Paul's day that we can have many teachers, but few fathers, it is truer today. Bill Johnson, his family, and his church are presenting a new model of ministry. Not the ministry of the professional minister, but the ministry of one who is intentionally becoming a "father" to many. Not just his family, church, and those who are a part of his School of the Supernatural, but now through his writings, conferences, and itinerate ministry he is becoming a "father" to many others.

This is an awesome book that will be added to my list of most important books for my interns to read, and for the students who will become part of the new missions school God has called us to start. I highly recommend it to all who want to be encouraged in their faith and in their relationship with God.

Randy Clark
Global Awakening Ministries
International Conference Speaker
Author, *God Can Use Little ol' Me*

FOREWORD

The operations of personal faith, though initiated by the Spirit of God in the human spirit, must be released with the permission of the mind. Therefore the mind must be transformed from the earthly, natural, and reasonable thinking that holds faith back to heavenly thinking that releases us to Kingdom living. The Kingdom of God is infinite and encompassing and the mind of man is challenged to "repent because the Kingdom of God is at hand" (Matthew 3:2). This challenge is a mandate to accept the eternal and infinite rule of God over everyone and everything for time and eternity. Nothing will deliver us from little thinking like the Kingdom of God.

Bill Johnson has done it again in lining up our human thinking with the mind of God and shocking us with the distance between the two.

A short while ago I wrote a commendation to Bill's first book, *When Heaven Invades Earth,* a scintillating challenge to Kingdom thinking with a report of repeated and continuing demonstrations of God's power documenting the results.

Here in this book with the equally appealing title, *The Supernatural Power of a Transformed Mind,* the author takes us to the next level of Kingdom thinking. After reading the first few pages I began to wonder what my life and ministry might have been had I been challenged with this information over half a century ago. I was discomforted by that line of thought, knowing that I could not go back and start over. After reading the next few pages I began to dream excitedly about what life and ministry are going to be because I have heard and seen what Bill Johnson so powerfully presents. This is not a book of theories about the reach of human abilities but a presentation of the mind and heart of God that is now working signs and wonders among His people.

Sound bites hammer at the reader's heart, presenting the gladdening possibility of immediate change. Reports encourage the mind to believe that what we have only read about in the Bible or heard reported from distant days, is really happening today. Here are a few of those sound bites:

"Most Christians have repented enough to get forgiven but not enough to see the Kingdom." Ouch! Wow! Repentance is associated in most of our minds with misery and regret; repentance unto "Kingdom vision" is encouraging and energizing!

"If your encounters with God don't leave you with more questions than when you started, then you have had an inferior encounter." Yes! Aren't you weary of the boredom that gathers around low expectations?

"The normal Christian life is perfectly poised between what we presently understand and the unfolding revelation that comes from the realm of mystery." Here we are challenged to "move on"! "Large numbers of Christians are practical atheists who disbelieve in an active God." We refuse to say in our churches today that there is no God but by our actions we are saying, "There is no God like the God of the Bible, nor do we want such a God!"

Finally Bill asks, *"Aren't you weary of talking about a Gospel of power and seeing no demonstrations of it?"*

Yes, Bill we are, we really are! And you have helped us by causing us discomfort with status quo and pointing to the way of repentance to Kingdom thinking.

The reading of this book may be dangerous to your present lifestyle but may become the most life-changing book you have read this year...or, for that matter, this decade. Enjoy the journey!

Jack R. Taylor, President
Dimensions Ministries
Melbourne, FL
Author, *The Key to Triumphant Living*
and *The Word of God with Power*

INTRODUCTION

This book is an attempt to address a very abused subject —*the mind of the believer.* On one hand the mind has been cast off by some creating a mindless gospel that is emotionalism at best, and cultic at worst. They delight themselves in doing things without reason, thinking that only then is God pleased by their great faith. On the other hand there are those who have elevated the mind above its rightful place, creating gospel that has reduced God to the powerless image of man. This group lives in the illusion that they are spiritually safe because they only accept the things they understand, raising carnal Christianity to an elite status. They unknowingly embrace the very deception they hoped to avoid. The challenge before us is to give ourselves completely to the full purpose of God for the mind of man through the model that Jesus gave us, thereby giving us access to His supernatural life style.

I have purposed to use every message, whether spoken or in print, to sow into the coming reformation. That is my cause —that the kingdoms of this world would become the kingdoms of our Lord. This book is intended to be one small step in that direction.

This book is a continuation of my first book, *When Heaven Invades Earth.* You do not have to read that one to benefit from this one, although it is recommended.

Chapter 1

Change Your Mind

It is unnatural for a Christian to not have an appetite for the impossible.

It had been an awesome Sunday night in the presence of God. When it was all finished—the prayer and praise, the teaching and the time of asking God for miracles—one of my staff members walked from the sanctuary into the hallway and saw a man jumping up and down saying, "Oh my gosh, oh my gosh!" His pants seemed too big for him—he was holding them up so they wouldn't slump around his ankles. He was puzzled, but knew God must have done something. When we asked around we learned that the man had been healed that night after receiving prayer. The tumors he'd come in with had instantly disappeared. He'd come all the way from a neighboring state because doctors had given him only two weeks to live. In his mind, we were his last stop on the way to heaven or on the way to a miracle. He came into the sanctuary where he continued to jump up and down with great joy, very much healed and very much in need of a new wardrobe.

How did it happen? The Kingdom of God had come crashing into his infirmity and overwhelmed it. It was another great night and another great victory over the enemy.

That same weekend a woman drove to our church from two states away because she was having difficulty breathing. The doctors had found what they believed was lung cancer. Her family had to help her into the building. After receiving prayer, she left pain-free, able to breathe without any restriction.

Again, Kingdom reality vanquished earthly affliction.

A NEW NORM...

Is that normal? Absolutely! But is it common in today's church? Not yet. But God is changing the way Christians think about the so-called impossible. He is teaching us to work hand-in-hand with the Kingdom so the reality of heaven comes crashing into earthly problems and overwhelms them. The results are astonishing miracles, great victories over the enemy, healing, deliverance, revelation, and more. It's not hype; it's not baseless hope or theory. It's fact. The two stories I shared above are actual situations in which affliction was completely vanquished by Kingdom reality, and there are many more I will share throughout this book. Many churches see the miraculous happen on a weekly, even a daily, basis. As you can imagine, it's a revolutionary approach to Christian living—a return to the authentic.

I wish I could say I have always lived in the everyday miraculous, but I haven't. I've been a pastor for decades, but I didn't see miracles for most of that time. I believed in healing and deliverance, but neither I nor the people I led prayed for them with any success. We had correct doctrine, but not correct practice. However, a number of years ago God began to take us on a journey, giving us fresh Kingdom eyes to see what normal Christian living ought to be. Having missed much of the main activity of the Kingdom for so long, we were eager to get back to the original plan of God on this earth. It has been a wonderful learning experience!

THE WILL OF GOD REALIZED...

I have come to see that the normal Christian life means miracles, spiritual intervention, and revelation. It means peace, joy, love, a sense of well-being and purpose[1]—all these traits that elude so many Christians. Written into the spiritual DNA of every believer is an appetite for the impossible that cannot be ignored or wished away. The Holy Spirit, the very Spirit that raised Jesus from the dead, lives in us, making it impossible for us to be content with what we can only see, hear, touch, taste, and smell. Our hearts know there is much more to life than what we perceive with our senses; we are spiritually agitated by the lack of connection with the realm of the supernatural. In the end, nothing satisfies the heart of the Christian like seeing so-called impossibilities bow their knees to the name of Jesus. Anything less than this is abnormal and unfulfilling.

Bad teaching and disappointment have robbed many people of this reality. But in these last days the Man of Understanding[2]— Jesus Christ, our Wisdom[3]—is drawing the deep things out of the hearts of His people, bringing them into the open. These things are the irrevocable callings of God.[4] We live in an unprecedented hour where people are hungering for and stepping into their destiny in great numbers, fulfilling the purpose of God for mankind on earth. It's an amazing, unprecedented time to be alive, and you and I get to be part of it!

To be effective believers, we must go well beyond the Christian life we have known. We must redefine "normal" Christianity so it lines up with God's idea of normal, not the definition we have accepted and grown accustomed to based on our experiences (or lack thereof). The normal Christian life begins with the realization that we were put here to do the will of God on earth as it is in heaven—and what a joy it is to participate in that. The problem I see as I travel and speak with other believers is that many people are confused about the will of God on earth. Like me, they've often heard people use the phrase "the will of God" in Christian circles, but the concept remained fuzzy and vague. For most of my life I have heard people talk about seeking the will of God for their church, or their personal life, or their career. Many of us have treated the will of God as if it's unknown or unknowable. Sincere believers might pray for days and weeks, looking more somber and beat-up all the time, and they'll tell you they're trying to find the will of God on a matter. I have done this, too! But the will of God is simpler and plainer than we have thought. In what is known as the Lord's Prayer, Jesus said clearly and concisely:

> *Our Father in heaven, hallowed be Your name. Your kingdom come. Your will be done on earth as it is in heaven* (Matthew 6:9-10).

The will of God is simply this: "On earth as it is in heaven." Isn't that basic? Isn't it refreshing? When we pray, "Thy kingdom come, Thy will be done," we're praying for the King's dominion and will to be realized right here, right now. That is a life-transforming, paradigm-shattering way to "do" normal Christianity. God has not kept His desires secret: He wants the reality of heaven to invade this rebel-torn world, to transform it, to bring it under His headship. What is free to operate in heaven—joy, peace, wisdom, health, wholeness, and all the other good promises we read about in the Bible—should be free to operate here on this planet, in your home, your church, your business, and your school. What is not free to operate there—sickness, disease, spiritual bondage, and sin—should not be free to operate here, period. That, in a nutshell, is our assignment as believers on earth, and that is what my church and certainly many others in the Body of

Christ are working toward with more focus and energy than ever before. We are out to destroy the works of the devil.[5] It's an awesome way to live!

When we make this our primary understanding of God's will, the other areas that trouble us so much will seem to sort themselves out.[6]

What happens when we make this our mission? Lives are set free, bodies are restored, darkness lifts from people's minds, the rule of the enemy is pushed back in every way imaginable. Businesses grow healthy, relationships flower again, people re-connect with their calling and purpose in life, churches grow, and cities feel the effects of having the Kingdom flourishing within them. Energy is freed up for Kingdom works in ways I have never seen before. Things happen regularly that are so extraordinary it's like stepping into the pages of a good novel. But it's not a made-up lifestyle; it's the lifestyle for which we were made.

A PRACTICAL INVASION...

A young man named Brandon, who is a graduate of Bethel School of Supernatural Ministry[7], was visiting friends in Washington State. They were at a restaurant and the waitress came to take their order. Brandon began to perceive things in his heart about the woman, and he shared them with her. They pertained to her relationship with her mother. The waitress was amazed, and she became so emotional that she had to take a break.

While the waitress was away, Brandon noticed an Asian couple staring at him from across the room. The woman had wrist braces on because she suffered from carpal tunnel syndrome, and one of her hands was completely frozen in a fist. Brandon walked over and asked if he could pray for her. She said that they were Buddhist, but they were willing to receive prayer. He prayed for her and she was healed on the spot. The whole family was instantly overjoyed and began praising Jesus, right at their table. They said they had been praying to their ancestors for a long time for her hands to be healed, but the prayers hadn't worked. Brandon explained who Jesus is, and they received the gospel with wonder and thankfulness. He went back to his table and for the rest of the evening, the healed woman sat there opening and closing her hand in amazement.

About that time, the waitress came back and asked if she could talk with Brandon outside. She was understandably confused and yet eager, and wanted to know more about God. Brandon shared further insight that the Holy Spirit gave him about her life and told her about Jesus' love. She gave her heart to the Lord and was filled with the Holy Spirit right there. She was breathless with excitement and declared she was going to tell all of her friends what had happened.

That sounds like something out of the Bible, but it is another very recent display of God's love from a normal Christian like you and me. It happens regularly to a whole company of believers. He simply made himself available to carry out God's will in the here and now. He didn't just share doctrine; he offered proof of who God is.

Proving the Will of God...

One of the major functions of miracles and supernatural living is to offer immediate, irrefutable proof of what God wants to happen on earth. It demonstrates who God is by showing what His reality looks like. The apostle Paul put it this way,

> *And do not be conformed to this world, but be transformed by the renewing of your mind,* ***that you may prove what is***

that good and acceptable and perfect will of God (Romans 12:2, emphasis mine).

Has it ever occurred to you that one of your jobs on earth is, like Brandon, to prove the will of God? To show other people what He is like? To allow Him to overwhelm the enemy's works through you? Most people don't know how God behaves, or what's inside His heart for each one of us. Your calling and my calling as believers may be too massive to fully understand, but the Bible's command is clear: Our job is to demonstrate that the reality that exists in heaven can be manifested right here, right now. We are not just to be people who *believe* the right things about God, but people who *put the will of God on display*, expressing it and causing others to realize, "Oh, so *that's* what God is like." Healing and deliverance and restoration do much more than solve the immediate problem; they give people a concrete demonstration of who God is.

One young man from our church was summoned for jury duty. I doubt they'll ever ask him again! While he was serving, a gang member got saved and three people were healed, one of them in front of a mocking crowd. This young man had so boasted in the Lord that many of the other jurors were publicly making fun of him. So he turned to an afflicted person, prayed, and the person was healed. The crowd went silent. Another man in a wheelchair stood before the people in the courthouse, moving his hands and displaying the healing power and love of Jesus Christ.

Some of our staff, along with students from our ministry school, have gone a number of times to a nearby university that is a major center of New Age spiritualism. The most popular religion on campus is witchcraft. My senior associate, a wonderfully anointed prophet of God, was invited to speak in a class on Christianity and the supernatural. He stood before the students and shared a brief testimony. At the end of the a young lady who was tormented by demons began to manifest under their influence. Kris commanded them to leave, and she was delivered in front of many wide-eyed students! She was then filled with so much joy that they had to carry her out of the classroom into the parking lot so the next class could begin. The students from both classes looked on at what was happening, stunned and dumbfounded. My associate began to call people out, pointing at them and speaking strong prophetic words into their lives that touched the secret things of their hearts. Some dropped to the floor instantly as if they'd lost their strength. Others sat there with their mouths gaping. "I saw you being dedicated to God," he told one young man who was the only unbeliever in a large family. And on it went until those witches and warlocks who had devoted their lives to the powers of hell knew there was a mighty God in Israel, and in the Church!

During worship one morning at our church, a woman who had esophageal cancer felt the fire of God come upon her. She turned to her husband and said, "God healed me." They went to the doctor and the doctor said, "This kind doesn't go away." But he examined her anyway and told her in complete astonishment, "Not only is it gone, you have a brand new esophagus."

During another service we were reading the Bible, and a man in the congregation suddenly couldn't see the words clearly. Everything went blurry. He didn't figure out why until he got home and took off his glasses and could see fine without them. God healed his vision without anyone praying for him. The same thing happened to a pastor at a conference who was enjoying the presence of God, and when he opened his eyes, he didn't need his glasses anymore.

RETURNING TO OUR PRIMARY MISSION...

Those are great examples of carrying out our original calling as human beings. Remember that God's first commission to mankind was,

> *Be fruitful and multiply; fill the earth and subdue it; have dominion over the fish of the sea, over the birds of the air, and over every living thing that moves on the earth* (Genesis 1:28).

He said those words to Adam and Eve so they would extend the boundaries of His garden—representing His government, His will—to the ends of the earth. His idea was to have a planet engulfed in His glorious rule, with mankind flawlessly "proving the will of God" on earth as it is in heaven. It is a beautiful, breathtaking picture, and it remains God's goal for you and me, for the Church and for all of mankind. God has never wavered in what He wants for this planet and from you and me.

Of course, we know that the original plan got derailed, and that Adam forfeited the rulership God gave him over the earth, putting humanity into slavery to the enemy. Paul wrote,

> *You are that one's slaves whom you obey...* (Romans 6:16).

But God had a plan of redemption in place: Jesus would come to reclaim all that was lost. God told the evil one,

> *And I will put enmity between you and the woman, and between your seed and her Seed; He shall bruise your head, and you shall bruise His heel* (Genesis 3:15).

When that prophecy was fulfilled in the death and resurrection of Jesus Christ, God took back the authority man had given away and reclaimed our purpose on this earth. He gave us a clear field to run toward the original goal—and run with all our might. We, the Church, are called to extend His rule in this earthly sphere, just as Adam was called to do. We see this in each commission shown in the gospel: the commission of the 12, the commission of the 70 and the 72, and the Great Commission.[8] God gave the same instructions: In essence, "Go heal the sick, preach the good news, demonstrate who I am and what I am like. Extend My Kingdom!"

But too few of us today follow those precise instructions. We get caught up in side arguments, intellectual skirmishes, theories, and emotional head-trips. We become enamored of our own talents and spiritual giftings, thinking we can direct our own course simply by putting our gifts and talents to use as we see fit. Though well-intentioned, we become self-appointed in our commissions, honestly believing we are submitting to God. In reality, it isn't possible to prove the will of God on earth as it is in heaven unless we are completely plugged into the primary mission God gave us. We put it this way: *There is no CO-missioning without SUB-mission to the primary mission.*

So what is the primary mission? We saw it before in the life of Jesus and in the testimony of Scripture. First John 3:8 states clearly that through intimacy with God, we are to *destroy the works of the devil.*

> *For this purpose the Son of God was manifested, that He might destroy the works of the devil* (1 John 3:8b).

That was Jesus' assignment; it was Adam and Eve's assignment; it was the disciples' assignment. Believers, *that is your assignment as well.* God's purpose in saving you was not simply to rescue you and let you keep busy until He shipped you off to heaven. His purpose was much bigger, much more stunning: He commissioned you to demonstrate the will of God, "on earth as it is in heaven," transforming this planet into a place radiant and saturated with His power and presence. This is the very backbone of the Great Commission, and it should define your life and mine.

BRINGING CONFLICT TO THE STREETS...

In our school of ministry we train people in signs and wonders, and are especially keen to learn how to operate in the supernatural outside the four walls of the church. We encourage our students by giving them specific assignments to invite God to work in public places. One day after class a bunch of students from our Worship School went to visit a lady in the hospital. She had a brain tumor, was deaf in one ear, and was losing feeling on the right side of her body. She spoke with great difficulty, slurring her words, and she was in terrible pain. Instead of laying hands on her and praying, the students surrounded her in worship, singing songs, expressing their love to the Lord. Pretty soon the woman said, "My ears opened!" The deafness had left. They kept singing and she said, "My speech is clearer!" She started speaking clearly. Pretty soon she was moving her limbs around. She exclaimed, "All the pain is gone!" God overhauled her body when a worship service broke out around her.

When we do the will of God, we bring Kingdom reality crashing into the works of the devil. We initiate conflict between earthly reality and heavenly reality, becoming the bridge and connection point that makes it possible through prayer and radical obedience to assert the rulership of God. Not long ago, a woman with a broken arm came to our church with her wrist in such pain that we couldn't even touch her skin to pray for it. We held our hands away and prayed, and within moments God healed it completely. She had no pain and was twisting the wrist all around. The arm was totally different than it had been seconds earlier. Kingdom reality had overwhelmed one of the devil's works. *That's* the normal Christian life I'm talking about.

Some of our local church leaders had a Native American reconciliation event and many more people showed up than were expected. We only had four salmon to feed about 900 people. But those four salmon fed everybody full to the brim, with leftovers! That's not possible in the natural, but it is in the normal Christian life.

Besides the weekly feeding of the poor, we have an annual holiday feast, in which families from the church adopt a table in our gym and decorate it with Christmas decorations. The tables are set with our finest china, crystal, and silverware. We then bus the needy to this event held in their honor. This past year we served prime rib. We started with 34 roasts to feed two seatings of about 500 people each. After serving 19 roasts in the first seating we realized that the 15 we had left were not enough for the 200 workers plus the second group of 500. The decision was made to not feed the workers. But when they went back into the kitchen there were 22. Seven more had mysteriously appeared. The workers were then fed, as was the second group of needy people. That should have exhausted our mysterious 22 roasts, but there were 12 more left after everyone had eaten! Multiplying bread is great, but I really like seeing prime rib multiply!

Aren't you tired of talking about a gospel of power, but never seeing it in action? Aren't you tired of trying to carry out the Great Commission without offering proof that the Kingdom works? Too many of us have been like a vacuum cleaner salesman who comes to the door and throws a handful of dirt in on the floor and says, "I represent the new Whiz Bang vacuum cleaner company. My vacuum cleaner is so strong that you have to remove pets and small children from the room. It sucks up everything in sight." But instead of demonstrating the vacuum cleaner he simply hands you a brochure (tract), promises that the machine will work, and walks away. That's cheating people! Yet that's often how we preach the gospel. We tell people how great the product is, but seldom demonstrate or prove it. It's like saying, "Hi! My name is Bill Johnson. I represent the King and His Kingdom. He heals all your diseases, delivers you from all your torments, and gets rid of the messes in your life. I can't show you how, though. You'll just have to believe it. So long."

Don't you think we have improperly defined how the Kingdom of God operates, missing the bulk of what Jesus taught? Some people teach that the Kingdom of God is for some time in the distant future or past, not here and now. Some consign all the promises of God in the Bible to the millennium or to eternity because the accepted wisdom is that we're going to barely make heaven. But Jesus taught and demonstrated that the Kingdom of God is a present-tense reality— it exists now in the invisible realm and is superior to everything in the visible realm. In the same way that Jesus is fully God and fully man, so the Kingdom is fully now and fully then. He spent His ministry showing us how to bring Kingdom power to bear on the works of the devil. *Our ministry should do the same.* We can't be self-commissioned, relying on our ministry gifts to carry out the Great Commission. We can't afford to work apart from the supernatural intervention of Kingdom reality. Our assignment has never been about what we can do for God, but what can God do through us. That is the essence of the gospel: to do exactly what Jesus did and destroy the works of the devil.

That is normal Christianity. Miracles are normal. Salvation and deliverance are normal. Revelation, prophetic insight, and words of knowledge are normal. But to return to that original mission, we must radically change the way we think. We must *repent* and *renew our minds.*

RENEWING THE MIND...

The only way to consistently do Kingdom works is to view reality from God's perspective. That's what the Bible means when it talks about renewing our minds. The battle is in the mind. The mind is the essential tool in bringing Kingdom reality to the problems and crisis people face. God has made it to be the gatekeeper of the supernatural.

To be of any use to the Kingdom, our minds must be transformed. We find a clue to what that word means in the transfiguration of Jesus when He talked with Moses and Elijah. The reality of heaven radiated through Jesus, and He shone with incredible brilliance. His body revealed the reality of another world. The word *transformed* in that passage is the same word we find in Romans 12:2. The renewed mind, then, reflects the reality of another world in the same way Jesus shone with heaven's brilliance. It's not just that our thoughts are different, but that our way of thinking is transformed because we think from a different reality—from heaven toward earth! That is the transformed perspective. The renewed mind enables His co-laborers to prove the will of God. We prove the will of God when put on display the reality of heaven. The unrenewed mind, on the other hand, brings about a completely different manifestation:

> *Hear, O earth! Behold, I will certainly bring calamity on this people—The fruit of their thoughts, because they have not heeded My words nor My law, but rejected it* (Jeremiah 6:19).

I understand that there is often hesitancy when we talk about the mind as a tool of God. At times in church history the intellectual aspect of the mind has been so exalted that it has wiped out a real lifestyle of faith. Men of sincere faith have been lured into a mindset of skepticism and doubt. Theology has been exalted at the expense of belief. Academic assessment has replaced firsthand, supernatural experience. There is good reason not to let the mind dictate how we will believe. But Christians often react to error and create another error in the process. Pentecostals have often downplayed the mind's importance, implying that it has no value at all.

Many Christians instinctively distrust the mind, thinking it is irredeemably corrupt and humanistic. They point to Harvard and Yale and other universities that were originally founded on Christian principles, but which today promulgate deceptions and lies. However, the mind is actually a powerful instrument of the Spirit of God. He made it to be the gate-keeper of Kingdom activity on earth. The great tragedy when a mind goes astray is that God's freedom to establish His will on earth is limited. The mind is not to be tossed out; it is to be used for its original purpose. If the mind weren't vitally important to our walk with Christ and our commission, Paul wouldn't have urged us to "be transformed by the renewing of our minds." In fact, only a renewed mind can consistently bring Kingdom reality to earth.

Yet many of us live with unrenewed minds, which are of little use to God. An unrenewed mind is like a discordant key on a piano. Once you discover that key, you don't use it anymore because it detracts from the music. You skip over it and work around it. In the same way, people who are out of sync with the mind of Christ seldom get used, no matter how available they are, because their thoughts conflict with the mind of Christ. They are self-appointed in their mission and are not in submission to the primary mission. As a result, they are working entirely outside God's intended commission.

However, when we come into agreement with the primary mission, our minds become powerful tools in God's
hands. This explains why there is such an intense war being
waged for your mind and your mental agreement. Every
thought and action in your life speaks of allegiance to God or
to satan. Both are empowered by your agreement. Renewing
your mind means learning to recognize what comes from hell,
and what comes from heaven, and agreeing with heaven. That
is the only way you will complete your divine assignment. God
designed your mind to be one of the most supernaturally powerful tools in the universe, but it needs to be sanctified and
yielded to the Holy Spirit so you can carry out His designs,
creative ideas, and plans in your everyday life.

REPENTANCE MADE PRACTICAL...

Renewing the mind begins with repentance. That is the
gateway to return to our original assignment on earth. Jesus
said, "Repent, for the kingdom of heaven is at hand."[9] To
many Christians, *repent*[10] refers to having an altar call where
people come forward and weep at the altar and get right with
God. That is a legitimate expression of repentance, but it's
not what the word repentance means. "Re" means to go back.
"Pent" is like the penthouse, the top floor of a building. Repent, then, means to go back to God's perspective on reality.
And in that perspective there is a renewal, a reformation that
affects our intellect, our emotions, and every part of our lives.
Without repentance we remain locked into carnal ways of
thinking. When the Bible speaks of carnality, it doesn't necessarily mean obvious, disgusting sin. Most Christians have no
appetite for sin; they don't want to get drunk or sleep around,
but because they live without the demonstrated power of the
gospel, many have lost their sense of purpose and gone back
to sin. Having a renewed mind is often not an issue of whether

or not someone is going to heaven, but of how much of heaven he or she wants in his or her life right now.

Jesus urged us to do an about-face in our approach to reality because His Kingdom is at hand. He brought His world with Him, and it's within our reach. He wants you to see reality from God's perspective, to learn to live *from* His world *toward* the visible world. But if you don't change the way you think, you'll never be able to apprehend the Kingdom power that is available.

Jesus said that "unless one is born again, he cannot see the kingdom of God" (John 3:3). What does that mean? Well, Jesus was not saying that we would have visions of heaven, though I know that happens. He was speaking more practically. He was saying that when our minds are renewed, we will see the Kingdom displayed and proven as He did in His earthly ministry. That's what it means to "see" the Kingdom of heaven. Our souls long to see such things. We have inside of us an unrelenting hunger to watch the Kingdom break into this realm—and not just to watch but to participate, to become the connecting point and gateway for God's power.

I walked into church one recent Sunday morning, greeting people before the meeting, and in the back I met a homeless gentleman who'd come as a guest of someone else. He had a cast on his arm and was treating it with great care. So I said, "Hey, what happened to your arm?"

He said, "I fell off a 20-foot bridge and shattered my wrist."

"How about if we pray for that?" I asked.

"Okay," he replied.

We prayed and I told him, "Now move it around."

He moved it and his jaw dropped. He looked in complete astonishment at the lady who brought him because he had been completely healed in a moment of time. His wrist was fine. When the invitation came for people to give their lives to Christ later in the service, he was the first to come forward. Once again we see that "His kindness leads us to repentance."[11]

That is a simple, everyday example of proving that the Kingdom works on earth. It is not mind-over-matter, or something spooky and weird. It is going back to God's perspective of reality and living as if we really believe it. His purpose—His reality—is to raise up a delegated group of people who work with Him to destroy the works of the devil, who demonstrate and prove the will of God here on earth as it is in heaven. That is the core of the Great Commission, and it is your privilege and mine to co-labor with Him in it.

PAUL'S REPENTANCE...

Most Christians have repented enough to be forgiven, but not enough to see the Kingdom. They go part of the way, then stop. Did you know that meeting Jesus was only the first step in your Christian walk? Conversion puts you at the entrance of an entirely new way of living, but there is a lifetime of experiences beyond the entrance that many folks don't experience. They never enter into their full purpose. They spend their life rejoicing just on the other side of the river shore, but never move in to take the cities and inhabit the promised land. It's not enough to barely make it across the river into the promised land; we must go all the way and fight for the territory God has promised to His Church.[12] Life is so much fun when we experience the miraculous and partner with the supernatural! It's an honor and privilege and responsibility that too many of us have feared and ignored.

The idea of Kingdom power and spiritual conflict unsettles some people, but without power, the gospel is not good news. Jesus never made the gospel simply a doctrinal exercise. That's why Paul was so concerned about properly presenting the gospel that he changed his way of doing ministry between one assignment and the next. You recall he was in Athens, preaching the gospel at Mars Hill where philosophers gathered to talk. They loved to exchange ideas and debate intellectual ideas of the day, but their talks were mostly meaningless and void of power or truth. Paul came into their midst and gave a brilliant message that is honored to this day by Bible schools around the world for its conciseness.[13] Then he gave an opportunity for people to come and to meet Jesus—and only a small handful of people got saved.

What a disappointment! This was, after all, the apostle Paul, who stirred up entire cities with the message and power of God, who was tossed in jail for disturbing the peace. Later, in Ephesus, the city was absolutely turned upside-down by his teaching and the demonstration of God's power. All the occult practitioners brought their piles of books and burned them spontaneously. There was massive repentance. Paul had also been to the third heaven, the realm of God, had seen things unutterable and impossible to describe. But when he went before this group of intellectuals and presented the gospel in a superbly intellectual way, there were very few converts. In fact, Acts 18:1 says, "After these things Paul departed from Athens and went to Corinth."

If Paul was like any other preacher I know, he had his share of *blue* Mondays where he rehearsed and re-evaluated the Sunday service a thousand times over, trying to figure out what he could have done better. As Paul was coming to Corinth, I believe he was evaluating his message, which was brilliant but had produced few converts. Looking ahead, he knew he would be preaching the gospel in Corinth. At this point, he actually described what he was thinking:

And I, brethren, when I came to you, did not come with excellence of speech or of wisdom declaring to you the testimony of God. For I determined not to know anything among you except Jesus Christ and Him crucified. I was with you in weakness, in fear, and in much trembling. And my speech and my preaching were not with persuasive words of human wisdom, but in demonstration of the Spirit and of power, that your faith should not be in the wisdom of men but in the power of God (1 Corinthians 2:1-5).

Some read this and conclude that Paul had a speech impediment or difficulty talking or lacked confidence before the crowds. I would suggest that it's none of those things. I think he was saying, "I ran an experiment with you. I decided not to tell you everything I knew because I wanted to make sure this time to leave room for the power of God. I didn't want you to put your faith in another man's gift. I didn't want you to be wowed by my words." Rather, as he said in verse 5, people's faith "should not be in the wisdom of men but in the power of God."

(I'm not saying that we shouldn't strive to teach well, or share in fullness the things that God has shown us. It's just that we shouldn't do any of these things at the expense of making room for God to show up and say "Amen" to His own word through the signs and wonders that follow.)

Notice that Paul didn't write, "I wanted your faith to be in the name of the Lord Jesus Christ." He used the phrase, "That your faith...[would be] in the power of God." Today there is a difference between preaching in Jesus' name and preaching with power. In Paul's day there was seldom a difference. Power was part and parcel of the gospel, as it should be for us in our everyday lives. Many of us have preached in the name of Jesus without any demonstration of power. That kind of powerless, ineffective preaching must stop. We can't afford to give the theory without the reality anymore. In fact, if Paul were on earth today he would warn against many of us because of how we rob the gospel of power. In First Corinthians 4:19-20, Paul warned new Christians against teachers who didn't demonstrate the power of God with their teaching. He was making a vital distinction; fathers move in power. Those who have only concepts and ideas are not presenting the full message of the gospel.

The gospel was presented in its wholeness, of course, in the life of Jesus who taught with power. Whenever He taught on the Kingdom, He would heal people. It wasn't one or the other; it was both. He told His disciples, "And as you go, preach, saying, 'The kingdom of heaven is at hand.' Heal the sick, cleanse the lepers, raise the dead, cast out demons" (Matt. 10:7-8). He showed us that proving the will of God means not only declaring the Kingdom is at hand, but demonstrating its effects.

A woman came to our church recently who had been in an accident and had five surgeries in just under five years. One of her arms was almost three inches shorter than the other, and she had no feeling in it from the elbow up. The doctor told her the damage was so extensive that the arm would dangle there the rest of her life. At the encouragement of her children, she came up for prayer. A woman laid hands on her, and the arm was healed and restored in a moment of time. Why? Because there are no arms like that in heaven. That infirmity had to leave because the Kingdom came upon her. She reached out to pick up her two-year-old girl, and the girl said, "No, Mommy, broken arm."

"It's okay, honey," the woman said. She picked her up, and there was a huge smile plastered on the girl's face—because for the first time in her life, her mommy was able to pick her up. *That's* the normal Christian life.

In the New Testament, the very word for salvation means healing, deliverance, and forgiveness of sin. The Kingdom brings the complete solution to the whole man, and we have access to that reality even now, just as Jesus did throughout His life.

Many believers think miracles and power are for extra-special anointed people of God. Many get hung up on the idea that Jesus did miracles as God, not man. In reality, as I said in my previous book[14] and I continue to remind people, Jesus had no ability to heal the sick. He couldn't cast out devils, and He had no ability to raise the dead. He said of Himself in John 5:19, "the Son can do nothing of Himself." He had set aside His divinity. He did miracles as man in right relationship with God because He was setting forth a model for us, something for us to follow. If He did miracles as God, we would all be extremely impressed, but we would have no compulsion to emulate Him. But when we see that God has commissioned us to do what Jesus did—and more—then we realize that He put self-imposed restrictions on Himself to show us we could do it, too. Jesus so emptied Himself that He was incapable of doing what was required of Him by the Father—without the Father's help. That is the nature of our call—it requires more than we are capable of. When we stick to doing only the stuff we can do, we are not involved in the call.

Jesus lived in constant confrontation and conflict with the world around Him, because Kingdom logic goes against carnal logic. This is a good time to ask yourself, are you living in conflict with this world? Are you bringing the reality of heaven, not just the doctrine of heaven, to your neighbors or coworkers? How is your life contradicting the way life works for most people in your city? How are you ushering in Kingdom reality wherever you go? A renewed mind sees the way God sees. It receives His impressions and becomes a creative force to release His expression of dominion on planet Earth.

A renewed mind destroys the works of the devil so that earthly reality matches heavenly reality. It proves the will of God not just in word but in deed. It heals the sick, frees those enslaved to sin, brings joy where there was sadness, strength where there was weakness, explosive creativity and world-changing ideas and inventions where there was lack of invention. It causes the Kingdom of God to be expressed "on earth as it is in heaven."

That's normal Christian living. And that's what we'll discuss in the coming chapters.

ENDNOTES

1. This does not mean there will not be troubles and persecutions. Those are also a part of the Christian life, as mentioned in the great chapter of faith: Hebrews 11. But even in those difficult times, which are the result of living righteous in an unrighteous world, enduring faith "overcomes the world."

2. Proverbs 20:5.

3. 1 Corinthians 1:30.

4. Romans 11:29.

5. 1 John 3:8.

6. Matthew 6:33.

7. This is our school to train people in the Christian lifestyle of the supernatural. Character/holiness is the bedrock of our training, yet we refuse to stop there.

8. Matthew 10, Luke 10, Matthew 28:18-20, respectively.

9. Matthew 4:17.

10. While this is not the actual etymological breakdown of the word, it does convey the principle the word represents.

11. Romans 2:4.

12. Exodus 23 and Joshua 1.

13. Acts 17.

14. *When Heaven Invades Earth.*

Chapter 2

Becoming the Dwelling Place of God

We were born to live under an "open heaven." Without that blessing we will fail to resource earth with heaven's resources.

My wife and I were at a service in Fortuna, California, with several others from our school and staff. Many local pastors were also in attendance. They, having embraced the message of the Kingdom, encouraged their congregations to participate. Healing was extremely easy that night.[1] Out of about 200 people there were approximately 40 to 50 who acknowledged that God had healed their bodies that night.

There was a woman with a destroyed optical nerve; the doctors had said that she would never see out of that eye again, but she was healed and can now see. A deaf person was also instantly healed that night, as was a woman bound to a wheelchair because of crippling arthritis. She danced and shouted, expressing the joy of her deliverance. Another wonderful miracle took place as our students prayed for a child with clubfeet. He also was healed. Because the leaders stood together in unity and love, the *miracle realm* was very easy to enter into.

A TIMELY REVOLUTION...

I am incredibly excited about the revolution I see taking place in the Church. We are again becoming the dwelling place of God that was promised in the Bible. We have hungered for more, prayed for more, and now we are receiving unprecedented insight into our privileges and responsibilities in the Kingdom of God. These insights aren't just being pondered; people are acting on them, and more and more, God's will is being done on earth as it is in heaven.

The Bible talks a lot about our being a dwelling place for God, and "God's house" on earth. What does it mean to be "God's house"? Why does this concept matter? How should it change the way we live our everyday Christian lives? What does it have to do with renewing our minds? The answer: It has everything to do with these things! Let's start by going back to the first mention of the House of God in the Bible. It's found in Genesis 28, which says,

> *Now Jacob went out from Beersheba and went toward Haran. So he came to a certain place and stayed there all night, because the sun had set. And he took one of the stones of that place and put it at his head, and he lay down in that place to sleep. Then he dreamed, and behold, a ladder was set up on the earth, and its top reached to heaven; and there the angels of God were ascending and descending on it. And behold, the Lord stood above it and said: "I am the Lord God of Abraham your father and the God of Isaac; the land on which you lie I will give to you and your descendants…. Then Jacob awoke from his sleep and said, "Surely the Lord is in this place, and I did not know it." And he was afraid and said, "How awesome is this place! This is none other than the house of God, and this is the gate of heaven!"…And he called the name of that place Bethel… (Genesis 28:10-13, 16-17, 19).*

Because this is the first mention in the Bible of the House of God, this passage defines the nature of this subject for the rest of Scripture. There are several aspects of this house that we should pay attention to. First, Jacob said, "God is here and I didn't even know it." This tells us that it is possible to be in the presence of the "House of God" (which we'll begin to define in a moment) and never know it's there. In other words, without a revelation—in Jacob's case, a dream—we can be oblivious to the presence and work of God in our lives or around us.

I have been in church services and meetings and have watched time and again as God transforms one person's life dramatically and utterly, but the person sitting next to him or her is clueless that God is even in the house. They're thinking of what they'll eat when they get home, while other people are having total spiritual reconstruction just a few feet away. I don't know how or why that works, but it happens all the time.

One of my former elders, Cal Pierce,[2] was a self-confessed "bored" board member when I came on as pastor. I had called for a special leadership meeting because of what God was starting to do in the church shortly after our arrival. It was obvious that I needed to introduce this new move of God to our leaders so they could actually "lead the charge." Cal did not like what was happening in the church and was attending the meeting out of duty. But God came upon him in one of the most sovereign acts I have ever witnessed. The Holy Spirit came upon him powerfully and apprehended him for a new work. If the Holy Spirit has claws, this man experienced them! God drafted him in a moment of time for something new. He was already born again, headed to heaven, but God had a purpose for his life that was much higher than he was experiencing. God shook off everything that had held him back. But as he was experiencing this spiritual transformation, there were many in that room who experienced and realized nothing.

They were like Jacob before his dream. God was there, and they didn't know it.

AN OPEN HEAVEN...

The other important thing about the House of God was that it functioned under an open heaven, meaning the demonic realm was broken off and there was clarity between the realm of God's dominion and what was happening on earth. It was pictured in Jacob's dream as a ladder with angels ascending and descending. Angels ascend when they've completed an assignment and descend when they're on their way to carry out a supernatural task.

(Let me add as a side note that I've often spoken and written about how I'm convinced that many angels have been waiting around for decades for Christians to live the risk-filled lifestyle God expects of us. Their job is to bring the reality of God's rule into situations that afflict and torment humans. Hebrews 1:14 tells us, "Are they not all ministering spirits sent forth to minister for those who will inherit salvation?" Angels are necessary to complete the assignment of the Lord. Psalm 104:3 says that God "walks on the wings of the wind." The wind is described as an angelic presence. God is actually ushered into a situation by *riding* on angelic presence. I would dare to say that you have never been involved in any supernatural activity except when the angels of the Lord were there to enforce and to help you carry out that assignment. A lifestyle without risks has little need for angelic assistance.)

Jacob awoke from his dream and declared that the place he was in was "none other than the house of God." What did he mean? He couldn't have meant a physical shelter because there were no buildings there, not even a little lean-to. He couldn't have meant the house of God was an organization, tribe, or religious group, because there weren't other people around. He probably was as confused as anyone what the dream meant, and as far as we know he didn't get the answer to his puzzling prophetic dream, though he must have wondered about it for the rest of his life. The answer arrived hundreds of years later in the person of Jesus, who was the initial fulfillment of this prophecy. John 1:14 says,

And the Word became flesh and dwelt among us, and we beheld His glory, the glory as of the only begotten of the Father, full of grace and truth.

Dwelt in this verse means "to tabernacle." Jesus *tabernacled* among us—He was the House of God made flesh—the place where God lived. He was the initial fulfillment of the prophetic picture in Genesis 28. The House of God was not a building, location, or denomination, but a Person. We see this illustration expanded later in the Gospel of John where,

Nathanael answered and said to Him, "Rabbi, You are the Son of God! You are the King of Israel!" Jesus answered and said to him, "Because I said to you, 'I saw you under the fig tree,' do you believe? You will see greater things than these." And He said to him, "Most assuredly, I say to you, hereafter you shall see heaven open, and the angels of God ascending and descending upon the Son of Man" (John 1:49-51).

The fulfillment of the House of God began with Jesus. He was the House of God on earth. But this concept did not stop with Him—far from it. He was the initial fulfillment of the House of God, but not the ultimate fulfillment. There is a big difference. For example, your conversion was not God's ultimate intent for you. It was His initial intent that set you up for the ultimate fulfillment, which is that you be filled with His fullness, living the normal Christian lifestyle as defined by what takes place in heaven. God's initial fulfillment of the

House of God was Jesus, the tabernacle of God on planet Earth. But then Jesus said to His disciples in John 14:16, speaking of the Holy Spirit,

And I will pray the Father, and He will give you another Helper, that He may abide with you forever.

Paul elaborated on this when he said in First Corinthians 3:16,

Do you not know that you are the temple of God and that the Spirit of God dwells in you?

And in Ephesians 2:19-22,

Now, therefore, you are no longer strangers and foreigners, but fellow citizens with the saints and members of the household of God, having been built on the foundation of the apostles and prophets, Jesus Christ Himself being the chief cornerstone, in whom the whole building, being fitted together, grows into a holy temple in the Lord, in whom you also are being built together for a dwelling place of God in the Spirit.

We, the Church, the redeemed, are the tabernacle of the Holy Spirit, the eternal dwelling place of God! We are living stones, according to First Peter 2:4-5, fitly framed together, building the eternal dwelling place of God. The House of God is *us!* Jacob's dream was not just about the Messiah but about you and me and every born-again believer throughout history. It is the heart of our very identity.

The House of God is the picture of God's intention for your life and for everything you do. He wants a house where He will dwell, where angels ascend and descend on assignment and the heavens are open over a people who abide in Him, meaning they stay connected in their affection and love for Him. God wants so much to invade this world with the reality of what was purchased on Calvary. But He waits for a people who will live the normal Christian life, putting themselves at risk, constantly tapping into the invisible resources of heaven that have been standing idle. That is how we function as the House of God.

If we understand and are confident in our identity as the House of God, we can do great exploits. No power of darkness in any realm of creation can stop our fellowship with the Father. There is an open heaven over each one of us, from the newest Christian to the most mature. Being the House of God means we have the exact authority Jesus has at the right hand of the Father. We are entitled and empowered to be His "House," His embodiment on earth. As a Christian at this very moment, you have absolute liberty and access to heaven.

I have been to many cities that are known for their darkness. Yet the practices of occult leaders cannot block the open heaven over any believer who abides in Christ. Even the demoniac, as tormented as he was, couldn't be stopped from his "God encounter" as he fell at Jesus' feet in worship! I never notice the lack of an open heaven, unless I become impressed with the devil's accomplishments in that city.

But some of our ladders have not been used in quite a long time. There are no angels coming or going because we haven't stepped into the area of the supernatural. That's our problem. To be the House of God, we must bustle and brim with the life, joy, healing, and peace that is normal in heaven. We must set our hearts on being a House filled with His glory wherever we go.

THE GATE OF HEAVEN...

Let's move from ladders and houses to gates, which are also mentioned in Genesis 28 and which pertain to our calling as the House of God. You'll remember that Jacob said, "This is none other than the house of God, and this is the gate of heaven!" (Gen. 28:17). Let's clarify up front that when talking about gates we aren't talking about a new path to salvation. Jesus referred to Himself elsewhere in the gospels as *the* gate (see John 10:9). He is the only door to salvation—there is no other way.

But in this context and elsewhere in the Bible, "gate" seems to mean a place of transition and access. In the natural you might walk through a gate to go from your front yard to the sidewalk, or from your backyard to your driveway. In the same way, when we talk about the Church being the gate of heaven, we are referring to the place where the reality of His dominion becomes available for all of mankind—His world invades ours!

Jesus talked about gates in Matthew 16:18-19:

> *...on this rock I will build My church, and the gates of Hades shall not prevail against it. And I will give you the keys of the kingdom of heaven, and whatever you bind on earth will be bound in heaven, and whatever you loose on earth will be loosed in heaven.*

The Church is the gate of heaven (another way of saying the House of God). Now Jesus introduced the idea of the gate of hell. When I was younger, I read this wrong somehow and thought it meant that "the gates of heaven will prevail against the assault of the enemy." That fit my theology better back then. I saw the Church as a group of people locked inside a compound, shoulders against the gate, trying to hold the fort as the devil and his powerful minions beat against it. I saw the Church in a posture of fear and weakness, trying to protect what we had until God hurried up and rescued us from the big, bad devil. But Jesus gave us an opposite picture. He said, "The gates of hell will not prevail." Has it ever occurred to you that we're on offense, not defense? The principalities and powers that set up dominions or "gates" all over the earth will not prevail against *us*! We are advancing and winning, and Jesus promises that in the end, no gate of hell will stand. Wow!

So where precisely are the gates of hell? Where does the devil sit in power? You'll recall from our discussion of renewing the mind that I called the mind the gatekeeper of the Kingdom of God. It is the place of access, transition, and power. It follows that the gates of hell are set up in *people's minds*. Jesus made this clear:

> *From that time Jesus began to show to His disciples that He must go to Jerusalem, and suffer many things from the elders and chief priests and scribes, and be killed, and be raised the third day. Then Peter took Him aside and began to rebuke Him, saying, "Far be it from You, Lord; this shall not happen to You!" But He turned and said to Peter, "Get behind Me, Satan! You are an offense to Me, for you are not mindful of the things of God, but the things of men"* (Matthew 16:21-23).

He didn't say, "Peter, you devil worshiper!" He didn't say, "You are filled with all kinds of occult practices and deceits." He said, "Your mind is filled with the things of man." A most important thing to remember is that the devil is empowered by human agreement! That mental posture was a gate from which satan was released to bring his destruction. To say, "I'm only human," is to say, "I'm only satanic." Humanity without Christ at the center is satanic in nature. When you've been given the Spirit of God, you lose the privilege of claiming, "I'm only human." You are much more than that! In fact Paul rebukes the church at Corinth for *behaving like mere men.*[3] Second Corinthians 10:5 confirms the location of the gate of hell when it says,

...bringing every thought into captivity to the obedience of Christ.

The gate of hell is in our minds any time we agree with the enemy. I empower him any time I agree with a man-centered perspective or natural wisdom that does not know God. I empower demonic forces and become a gate to release his power to kill, steal, and destroy in my life. It's chilling, but the Bible indicates it's a fact.

A GATEWAY PEOPLE...

Our goal, then, is to agree with heaven all the time, to let our minds be the gate of heaven where angels ascend and descend freely on assignment from God. It's not that they literally flow through our minds. It's just that they are released through our agreement. The original New American Standard Bible confirms this when it says,

Whatever you bind on earth shall have been bound in heaven, and whatever you loose on earth shall have been loosed in heaven (Matthew 16:19, NAS).

This was the entire focus of Jesus' ministry, and it's a great word of authority to us. Whatever we bind has already been bound. Our task is to see what is bound up there, and then bind it down here. Whatever is free in the heavenly realm to function needs to be released here. We are to be a gateway people for the free flow of heavenly realities into this planet.

Not long ago a woman came for prayer during one of our services. Her baby had died in the womb, but the person praying for her said, "The baby is not dead." This woman said, "Excuse me, I've already been to the doctor, they've taken the test, and they will remove the child next week." The person praying said, "The child is not dead. The Lord speaks to me, and He says the child is alive." This woman went back to the doctor and they were dumbfounded because the child that had been dead was now alive. The person praying had functioned under an open heaven. They became a gate, so that what was spoken by the Father in His throne room was carried out without hindrance by angels on assignment on earth.

I first heard about binding and loosing more than 25 years ago, and I began trying it out. A friend came to me who was in a court case and there wasn't any question that he would win, but it was devouring his money through attorney fees. The suit had been brought on by somebody who had the money and the intent to bring torment to my friend. This went on for months. We would meet together and pray, and I would bind that spirit of deception, but nothing happened. Then one day I heard a brother teach on this subject in a more complete manner. I had been binding what wasn't free to function in heaven, but I wasn't replacing it with anything. I met with my friend and said, "We need to pray again. I have been binding the spirit of injustice, but we need to loose the spirit of justice." We prayed together, binding the spirit of injustice, the demon of deception and accusation, and loosing into the situation a spirit of justice and revelation of truth. It was a simple, direct prayer. He called me within an hour notifying me that the court case had been dropped. From then on I have continued to see the same kind of result with binding and loosing. I began to learn, with small steps, how to be a gateway for heaven's reality to take over every part of my life, and the lives of people around me, no matter how big or small the specific situation was.

How do we know what is bound and loosed in heaven? Who tells us what heaven's reality looks like? The only way to know these things and to function as the House of God and gate of heaven is to have revelation of what is happening in heaven. Otherwise, we're working in the dark. God has always wanted to release truth to His people, backed by the Word, of things that are found in heaven but have no earthly parallel. In John 3:12, Jesus said:

> *If I have told you earthly things and you do not believe, how will you believe if I tell you heavenly things?*

He was expressing a desire to reveal things to us about what's happening in the spiritual realm that have no corresponding earthly picture. I am convinced that as His government and Kingdom rule increase on this earth, as it says throughout Scripture, "of the increase of His government there will be no end," and as this planet is engulfed in the glory of God, the Church will receive revelation like we've never known. We'll come into agreement with the Father for the release of unprecedented miracles and power, fulfilling our destiny of being the House of God, the gate of heaven.

But first we must learn to hunger for and receive revelation as part of our everyday lives. That revelation will help us to carry out our earthly assignments with greater precision and wisdom. We'll talk about revelation, and how to know what's happening in heaven, next.

ENDNOTES

1. Healing is always easy in the sense that "we don't do it—God does!" But sometimes it just seems to flow better than others. This was one of those nights.

2. Founder of the Spokane Healing Rooms, Cal tells his story more fully in his book, *Preparing the Way.*

3. 1 Corinthians 3:3.

CHAPTER 3

REVELATION AND
UNDERSTANDING

We thrive with prophetic revelation, but perish without it.

My Senior Associate, Kris, was on a flight from San Francisco to Redding. Seated next to his wife was a man they'd never met, named John. John was around six feet four, had a spike coming out of his chin, a goatee, and a tattoo of a satanic head. He was the bass player for a heavy metal band. Kris, who operates very strongly in the gifts of the Spirit, began to receive revelation about John, so he switched seats with his wife and struck up conversation. Soon, Kris was speaking directly into John's life. "Your father abandoned you," Kris said. "You look tough, but you really are a mama's boy. You love children and you feel like you are supposed to work with orphans." John was shocked by the accuracy of Kris's words. He continued by saying, "You've been thinking about marrying a particular woman. She's the right one. She will help you in these changes because she has the same heart as you do. You are going to leave the band next year and she will go with you to minister to orphans all over the world." Every area that Kris addressed had already been on John's mind. But when Kris spoke about them he discovered that God knew the secrets of his heart, and actually cared about his life.

John's life was changed from that point on because of the revelation that came to him in that conversation. Those things happen often with Kris and many others from our church. A few months before the John incident, Kris boarded another flight and sat next to someone who'd been divorced and was struggling in his relationships with his children. Kris spoke prophetically into his life, and counseled with him about forgiveness and releasing his kids to have relationships with his ex-spouse's new partner. After a while the man looked at Kris in amazement and said, "You have just given me the keys that I have been seeking for a year!" This was again, a very simple demonstration of God's love, seen through a willing servant.

That is the nature of revelation—it opens up new realms of living, of possibility, of faith. It is absolutely impossible to live the normal Christian life without receiving regular revelation from God. The Bible does not say, "My people perish for a lack of miracles," or lack of money, or because of bad relationships or bad worship leaders or insufficient nursery staff, or anything else we could list. It says, "My people are destroyed for lack of knowledge" (Hos. 4:6). Proverbs 29:18 says similarly, "Where there is no revelation, the people cast off restraint." A more correct and complete translation is: "Without a prophetic revelation, the people go unrestrained, walking in circles, having no certain destiny."

The biblical word *vision* doesn't mean "goals." Goals are fine, but this *vision* is referring to the spirit of revelation coming upon you, giving you a vision of things that are unseen. Revelation is so essential in our lives that without it we perish. This is not a nice vitamin pill we can take or leave. This is what we live by. Without unfolding prophetic revelation that expands your capacity to see life from God's perspective, you will

REVELATION AND UNDERSTANDING

perish. Without seeing your present circumstances through God's eyes, you will spiritually die. It is so vital that Paul wrote to the Ephesians—those who seemed to have their act together in every area, who experienced perhaps the greatest revival recorded in the New Testament—and said he prayed that God would,

> ...*give to you the spirit of wisdom and revelation in the knowledge of Him* (Ephesians 1:17b).

If the revival-steeped Ephesian church needed to be reminded of the importance of revelation, we need to hear it much more. Revelation is critical to the normal Christian life.

TUNING IN...

The problem is that many Christians don't tune in to God's revelation. Paul put it well when he wrote,

> *Now we have received, not the spirit of the world, but the Spirit who is from God, that we might know the things that have been freely given to us by God. ...But the natural man does not receive the things of the Spirit of God, for they are foolishness to him; nor can he know them, because they are spiritually discerned* (1 Corinthians 2:12,14).

Right now in the room where you're sitting, movies are playing all around you. If you had the right receiver or satellite dish, you could pick them up. Just because you can't see the waves passing through doesn't mean they aren't there. With the right receiver you could watch any number of television shows, ball games, talk shows, or listen to private conversations on cell phones and short wave radio. But without the proper receiver, you won't pick up anything.

Likewise, the Bible says the natural man does not *receive* the things of the Spirit of God. If God is speaking on FM radio and we are on AM, we can turn that dial all the way to the left, then go slowly over every station. We can quote verses with every turn of the dial. We can claim the promises of God. We can do anything we want to, but as long as we are on AM and He is on FM, we are not going to receive His message because the natural man is receiving. The key is to be spiritually discerning—to open our spirit man to direct revelation from God. The Bible says,

> But as it is written: "Eye has not seen, nor ear heard, nor have entered into the heart of man the things which God has prepared for those who love Him." But God has revealed them to us through His Spirit. For the Spirit searches all things, yes, the deep things of God (1 Corinthians 2:9-10).

The Holy Spirit searches for things that have never been heard by human ears or seen by human eyes. He is the greatest search engine in the whole universe. Talk about quick and accurate! He searches the greatest reservoir of information imaginable—the heart of the Father. Psalm 139:18 says that God's thoughts about each one of us outnumber the sands on every seashore on this planet, and according to Jeremiah 29:11, all those thoughts are for your welfare, benefit, and blessing. God has been around a long time, and He has had a long time to think about you. He's been living in the experience of knowing you long before you were ever born. He doesn't just have a few random thoughts about you here and there. For trillions of years, God has been thinking about you, and the Holy Spirit searches that whole archive and brings incredible treasures to you at precisely the right moment—if you're listening.

RECOGNIZING REVELATION...

You'll know when He is speaking because it will have a freshness to it. It will always be better than anything you could have thought up yourself. And if He gives you new ideas, they will probably be impossible for you to accomplish in your own strength. His thoughts will so overwhelm you that you'll want to draw close to Him so they can be accomplished.[1]

Most born-again people know what it's like to be in confusion or trouble and have someone speak a word that brings a supernatural invasion of peace into their soul. You might not even have all of the answers you thought you needed five minutes ago, but for some reason, you don't care. Their words were the spirit of revelation from God Himself. The same way that Jesus became flesh, the Holy Spirit becomes words, and when they are spoken, they bring life.[2] We don't even have to comprehend it to embrace it. We just have to wrap our hearts around it and eventually it will start making sense.

Proverbs says *knowledge is easy to a man of understanding* (see Prov. 14:6). Some people get torrents of revelation and others don't. There are a couple of reasons why. First, it depends on how we build our support structure. There are pillar truths in the gospel that form the most basic foundation of the structure. Once you have these in place, God delightfully adds to them, as a decorator decorates a house after the foundation and walls are secure. A man of understanding accepts God's additions and doesn't question them. He is not doubleminded about them. That's how a person of understanding attracts greater understanding. You treasure something that God says, and that builds a foundation for greater revelation.

Another way to attract revelation is to obey what we know. One man came to Jesus and asked what to do to gain eternal life.[3] Jesus said, "What does it say to do?" The man said, "Love the Lord your God with all of your heart and soul and mind and love your neighbor as yourself." Jesus said, "Do that and you will be fine" (my paraphrase). The man pressed Jesus for more, but Jesus wouldn't give him any new information. He pointed him back to what he already knew. The man's first responsibility was to obey the revelation he had. Until he walked in obedience, he wasn't going to get more.

Obedience is a signal to God that says, "God, I want to go the next step." That tender heart draws the spirit of revelation to a person and/or to a body of people; they begin seeing and hearing things they never heard or saw before. The Bible even says, "He will seal up that instruction in our heart in the night while we sleep" (Job 33:15-16).

REVELATION SETS THE BOUNDARIES...

Revelation is for every single believer, not just for some "gifted" folks. The greater revelation that a person carries, the greater faith he or she is able to exercise. If I believe it's not God's desire to heal everybody then my revelation limits me every time a person comes to me who is sick. I have to settle it in my heart—is it really God's will to heal people? As long as I shun the revelation that God wants everybody to be healed and whole, I have cut myself off from releasing faith in that area. Revelation enlarges the arena that our faith can function in. Deception shrinks our area of faith.

If you believe that only the Benny Hinns of the world can pray for the sick and get consistent success, then your faith will operate within the limits of that misconception. But what if Jesus' words come alive to you, as in Matthew 10 where He sent them out two by two and told them to heal the sick, raise the dead, cleanse the leper, and cast out devils? What if you realized that the lifestyle Jesus lived and taught is meant to be *your* lifestyle? Revelation would broaden the boundaries for your faith to operate in.

REVELATION ISN'T GIVEN CARELESSLY...

In Matthew 13, the disciples asked, "Why do You speak to them in parables?" and Jesus said,

Because it has been given to you to know the mysteries of the kingdom of heaven, but to them it has not been given (Matthew 13:10-11).

Revelation is not something you can dig out of a theological book or study guide. It's not even something you can unravel in the Bible all by yourself. Revelation is locked up in a realm the Bible calls "mystery." A mystery cannot be hunted down and trapped like an animal. It can't be discovered by persistent searching. It must be revealed. We don't unlock mysteries; they are unlocked for us. And they are only unlocked and revealed to those who hunger for them. Jesus said He concealed truth in parables so it remained a mystery to some, but not for others. In the same way He put gold in the rocks and said, "If you want it, go find it and dig it out." The Bible says,

It is the glory of God to conceal a matter, but the glory of kings is to search out a matter (Proverbs 25:2).

God doesn't take the pearls of revelation—those things that were gained through hardship and difficulty, conflict and irritation—and freely throw them out to anybody.

We cannot enter into revelation without the assistance of the Spirit of God. First Corinthians 2:6-8 confirms this when it says,

However, we speak wisdom among those who are mature, yet not the wisdom of this age, nor of the rulers of this age, who are coming to nothing. But we speak the wisdom of God in a mystery, the hidden wisdom which God ordained before the ages for our glory, which none of the rulers of this age knew; for had they known, they would not have crucified the Lord of glory.

Unfortunately, mystery is not something that most people in the Western world appreciate. We have this idea that God knows our address and if He wants us to have an insight or experience, He will send it to us. We don't want to work for it or hunger after it. The spirit of self-pity has found tremendous home in this culture, but self-pity doesn't attract a visitation of God. Faith does. Faith moves the economy of heaven. It is the very currency of heaven.

Mystery should be a continual part of your life. You should always have more questions than answers. If your encounters with God don't leave you with more questions than when you started, then you have had an inferior encounter. A relationship with God that does not stir up that realm of mystery and wonder is an inferior relationship. It would help all of us a great deal if we had to walk out of a few more church services, scratching our heads, wondering what just took place. He is the God of wonder, the God of awe! But tenderness of heart enables us to come into the realm of revelation that unlocks the mysteries of God.

Seeking Revelation...

Though we can't snap our fingers and cause ourselves to have revelation, we still must hunger for it and pursue it. Jeremiah 33:3 says,

> *Call to Me, and I will answer you, and show you great and mighty things, which you do not know.*

The word *mighty* is an Old Testament word that is similar to the New Testament word *mystery*. It's a picture of something that is out of reach, unattainable, behind fortification. God has hidden mighty and mysterious things *for* us, not *from* us. He has already allotted to us this mysterious realm of the Kingdom, but it doesn't come to just anyone. It comes to those who are open and hungry for it. Jeremiah used the word *call*, which means "to cry out to the Lord in a very loud voice." Picture a person desperate enough to open his or her heart fully and issue a deep cry from the spirit. That deep part of man calls to the deep part of God.[4] That opening of the heart determines the level of revelation we receive. Few people I know receive substantial revelations or visitations of God without reckless pursuit. Most people I know who receive revelation cry out day and night for that fullness of the Holy Spirit. Casual prayer gets casual revelation. Deep cries cause God to "hear you" and "answer you" and "show you great and mighty things you do not know."

This is the Old Testament equivalent of the promise of Ephesians 3:20 when it says,

Now to Him who is able to do exceedingly abundantly above all that we ask or think, according to the power that works in us.

First Corinthians 2:9 says,

Eye has not seen, nor ear heard, nor have entered into the heart of man the things which God has prepared for those who love Him.

Prayer—the desperate cry of the heart of man—initiates the beginning of revelation to your heart and mind.

Second Peter 1:2-3 put it this way:

Grace and peace be multiplied to you in the knowledge of God and of Jesus our Lord, as His divine power has given to us all things that pertain to life and godliness, through the knowledge of Him who called us by glory and virtue.

The spirit of revelation opens up our knowledge of who God is, and from that comes the release of power from heaven. That power gives us access to all things pertaining to life and godliness. That encounter with God will not only shape the world around you, it will shape the world *through* you.

73

The most revered people in the Old Testament were the prophets because of the spirit of revelation that came upon them. Kings feared them. They knew that they could do anything in secret and the prophets would know. The Bible even says, "Surely the Lord God does nothing, unless He reveals His secret to His servants the prophets" (Amos 3:7). And now that spirit of revelation is not limited to people with unique gifts. It is liberally given to anyone who will pursue and ask—including you.

Hosea 6 says that we press on to know the Lord, meaning we seek an encounter with God, a revelation that launches us into a new awareness of how life is to be lived.

Let us know, let us pursue the knowledge of the Lord (Hosea 6:3).

The cry of Hosea was, "Let's press on—no, let's hunt down and chase the encounter with God that changes our understanding of reality." That is the kind of relentless pursuit each believer should have about the things of God. We need revelation to renew our minds, to help us prove the will of God on earth as it is in heaven.

I can't live life knowing there are realms of mystery, and keys to those realms, that are available to me but which I have not yet discovered. I can't sit back and say, "If it's God's will, He can drop a revelation into my lap." I need more, constantly. My spirit is hungry for things I have not yet known. Sometimes I get around certain people whose gifts and personality are so different yet so complementary to mine that I get revelation so fast in conversation I wish I had a tape recorder with me at all times. I get knowledge that connects 15 other things I've been thinking about and ties them all together. Those are wonderful times.

And yet I know that as Christians, we will always live in tension between what we understand and what remains a mystery. Years ago a famous author made a comment on a series of books he had written saying, "I don't know what is wrong with them, but they are too perfect. They answer every question and remove the realm of mystery. So I know something is wrong."

We cannot afford to live only in what we understand because then we don't grow or progress anymore; we just travel the same familiar roads we have traveled all of our Christian life. It is important that we expose ourselves to impossibilities that force us to have questions that we cannot answer. It is a part of the Christian life, which is why the Christian life is called "the faith." The normal Christian life is perfectly poised between what we presently understand and the unfolding revelation that comes to us from the realm of mystery.

EXPANDING REVELATION...

This realm of mystery and revelation goes far beyond what we normally think of as "ministry." There are vast resources of revelation in heaven for the areas of education and business, the arts and music, and these resources have yet to be tapped anywhere near to their fullness. There are melodies that have never been played or considered. There is lyrical content that would minister deeply to the Church and stir the world to conversion. Our job is to tap the revelation of the Lord in our area of talent or gifting so that we can accurately and powerfully reflect the King and His Kingdom.

I'm convinced that the pace of revelation will increase very rapidly in these last hours of history. Amos 9:13 says, "the plowman [will] overtake the reaper," meaning the seasons won't be so distinct anymore. They will overlap so that planting and harvesting occur in the same motion. We will live in a supernatural season when understanding will come much more quickly and bear fruit much more dramatically. We already see acceleration in history in the development of technology, science, and medicine. The knowledge of man is increasing, but don't think for a moment that God will not do equally and more so for the Church in spiritual matters. He is looking for men and women of understanding. He is ready to add the plywood to the frame of understanding, but we've got to have the framing in place first. He is ready to put on the drywall and the decorations and release revelation to each of us in quantities we've not yet known.

That acceleration of revelation is beginning in our day. God is presently wooing people into intimacy so they know how He thinks and moves. People are coming alive to that wooing and, in the process, to their sense of destiny. It's not about the greatness or accomplishment of any particular person or church. It's about the purposes of God being unveiled on the planet. On-going revelation and encounters with the power of God launch us into understanding of things we've never understood before.

Presently, every denomination, church, and group seems to have revelation into certain Kingdom matters. Nobody has the whole picture; God refuses to give it all to one person or one group because He wants us to be interdependent members of one another. But in these last days God is going to release a Spirit of revelation over the Church where we repent over our areas of great difference because we see Him as He is, we hear His word as He declares it, and we are literally taught by the Spirit. We are coming into an hour where there will be a common revelation,[5] a time when, as the Bible says, "all shall know Him" (Jer. 31:34). I believe it is talking about an hour when the people of God will simultaneously hear and see similar revelations, no matter the group or church.

Let's be people of on-going, life-changing revelation from God. But let's never allow revelation to stop there. It must lead to direct, hands-on experience to have any effect at all. That's what we'll see in the next chapter.

ENDNOTES

1. The most important thing to remember on this subject is that He will never contradict His Word, the Bible.
2. John 6:63.
3. Luke 10:25-28.
4. Psalm 42:7.
5. Ephesians 4:13.

CHAPTER 4

UNDERSTANDING IS AN EXPERIENCE

We must require an experience from what we believe.

Following an extended time of ministry in Africa, a ministry team from our church went to Johannesburg, South Africa, before leaving the continent. They didn't confine ministry to a church service or a healing line; they were instantly ready wherever they went. After the main aspect of the trip was over, they were walking from their hotel to a restaurant, intending to relax and buy souvenirs, when they came across a homeless man named Peter who was in a wheelchair. Peter shared how he'd been paralyzed for 11 years after falling from a height of four stories. He couldn't feel anything from his waist down and could barely move his arms. The day before, local hoods had taken him to a field and left him to die. Peter had given up on life, but heard God say, "If you stay here, you're going to die." So he crawled all the way back to town using only his arms.

The team prayed for him and Peter's leg started shaking crazily. "What's happening to me?" he cried out. He began to weep and repent for being mad at God. He even promised to give up smoking. A team member went to buy shoes and socks, seeing that Peter would be walking soon. They put the shoes and socks on his feet, and he felt a tickle in his toes, the first sensation he'd had there for 11 years. They lifted him up and he began to walk. His countenance completely changed. The man who had pushed Peter's wheelchair for many years was saved, too, and they all sang together, "Our God is an awesome God."

That parking lot became the scene of spontaneous ministry as word quickly spread about Peter's healing. People stopped out of curiosity to observe what was happening, and soon they were saved and filled with the Holy Spirit. Then a car drove up, and the driver was impatiently trying to get past the crowd. Team members approached the car and discovered that one of its occupants had been the one who robbed Peter and left him in the field to die. That man got out of the back seat and fled from the scene. The other two saw how Peter was healed, and they gave their lives to Christ and broke off their witchcraft bands. In all there were around a dozen new Christians, some filled with the Holy Spirit, and a cripple who wasn't crippled anymore—all on the way to get a bite to eat!

That's called putting revelation into practice. You see, renewing the mind is not merely reading words on a page and having a moment of revelation about a particular verse. That passes for renewal of the mind in many churches, but at best that's only half the equation. Renewal comes as revelation leads you *into a new experience with God,* as those people had that day in South Africa. You may have a moment of inspiration while reading the Bible or listening to someone preach from the Scriptures, but without taking the next step into experience, the process stalls and there is no renewal.

Jesus put it this way in John 5:39:

> *You search the Scriptures, for in them you think you have eternal life; and these are they which testify of Me.*

This says clearly that revelation is meant to bring us into an encounter with God, and if it doesn't, it only makes us more religious. Revelation is never given to increase our head knowledge. That's a by-product, at best. We are probably all so "smart" in biblical things that we could drown in the flood of information! Some theologians read the Scriptures 12 hours a day and have no clue about the Kingdom of God. They can recite endless evidence of their knowledge, but there is nothing revelatory or transforming about their lives. That has happened to many Christians who have at times embraced a routine of reading Scripture without letting the reading lead to experience. To renew the mind we must not just *think* differently but *live* differently, in a new experience of the empowerment of the Holy Spirit.

REVELATION WITH FEET...

Three young people from our church were at an ice cream shop one evening when they suddenly felt the presence and power of God come upon them, almost like a burst of fire. Realizing that God was up to something, they looked around for an opportunity to participate in the impossible and they saw a young man on crutches. They approached him and struck up conversation. He said he had fallen from 15 feet in the air into 2 feet of water, breaking his tailbone. He didn't reveal it then, but he was a star running back at one of the local high schools. They prayed for him and suddenly he dropped his crutches and started jumping up and down. Then he took off running back and forth as fast as an athlete in competition. People in the parking lot stared in amazement and befuddlement. He kept yelling, "Praise God! Praise God! I've always wanted God to do something like this to me!" He was completely healed.

Those young people put into practice their revelation of God's power to heal. Instead of having a simple evening at the ice cream shop, they sought out an opportunity for God to do a miracle. That's how to put revelation to work!

When God reveals things to us, we must put those things to work. If we don't, we will lose the power and opportunity that revelation offers us. Jesus warned,

> *When anyone hears the word of the kingdom, and does not understand it, then the wicked one comes and snatches away what was sown in his heart* (Matthew 13:19).

The revelation of the Kingdom is often spoken of as a living seed of another world that carries with it new possibilities. But when a person hears the word but doesn't understand it, the enemy has open access to that seed and can snatch it away. In our culture, we define understanding as nothing more than cognitive reasoning, coming to conclusions, fully comprehending. But in Eastern culture, which is the culture of Scripture, understanding is an *experience*. It means engaging in activities that involve our five senses. In fact, the Greek word for *understanding* in this verse means "learning which takes place through the five senses." It means *doing*, as in *practical human experience*. The biblical view of understanding means far more than to give mental assent; it means to practice in real life what one has come to know by revelation. That's why the Jewish leaders said to Jesus,

> *Rabbi, we know that You are a teacher come from God; for no one can do these signs that You do unless God is with him* (John 3:2).

To understand also means yielding to something before you can explain, define, or describe it. Biblical understanding far surpasses the intellect. Hebrews 11:3 says, "By faith we understand that the worlds were framed by the word of God, so that the things which are seen were not made of things which are visible." We don't have faith because we understand, but we understand because we have faith. In other words, it is imperative to accept and understand things without completely satisfying your intellect. When I read the Bible, I don't always understand what I'm reading. Biblical learning takes place in the spirit first, and as we obey the Spirit of God, our spirit communicates it to our minds so we intellectually understand. But understanding is not required for obedience. A normal Christian is one who *obeys the revelations and promptings of the Holy Spirit without understanding.* Understanding usually unfolds in the experience.

To understand, we must obey revelations and put them into practice. As an example, let's say I speak to my church about caring for the poor, something we love to do. I may stand up on Sunday morning and do the best job I can to illustrate the plight and need of the poor. People all across the room may be moved in their emotions. But if they don't do something practical within the next two to three weeks—perhaps finding a poor family to help out, or volunteering at a soup kitchen—then that word is open to be taken from the heart, where it has the place to transform their lives. Revelation takes us only halfway there; experience leads us all the way. The great tragedy is that if you don't move into experience, that revelation remains locked in your mind so you think it's active in your life. The next time you hear a message about helping the poor you might say, "Amen. The other people in this room need to hear that," even though you have done nothing to help the poor. Hearing without doing has locked you into a form without power.

There are great audiences, great crowds of people, great denominations and movements that would fight to the death to defend divine healing, or prophecy, or many other practices, but they never see those things happen. They think, "I understand the concept. I agree that it happens. If it's God's will, He knows my address and He can give me that grace." They have the revelation, but can't point to any proof of its validity in their personal experience. They can't show anyone how to do it. Their mental concept insulates them from the conviction that anything more needs to happen. They develop anesthesia that deadens their sensitivity to personal transformation. They are robbed of experience and can only recite back principles. It is pure religion, form without power.

For example, Jesus said in John 3:13, "No one has ascended to heaven but He who came down from heaven, that is, the Son of man who is in heaven." Strange verse, isn't it? We tend to only think of heaven as a place that is out in space somewhere instead of a place that coexists with us. We have a difficult time comprehending and wrapping our hearts around this statement, and so we let it become a nice, encouraging statement with no practical application to our lives. What does it mean, the Son of Man who is *in* heaven? What does it say about our job here on earth? Doesn't it mean that, like Jesus, we should live in a posture of dwelling in heavenly realms and living toward the afflictions, infirmities, and difficulties of the world around us? Shouldn't we function as ambassadors of another world, living in the realm of faith, which is the realm of the Spirit, which is called "the kingdom"?

But most of us have not realized that we can demand that the truth become an experience. Revelation should change our hearts before we could ever explain what we learned. The Bible says we are, as a matter of fact, seated at the right hand of the Father in Christ Jesus in heavenly places. This was written for us to experience, not so we have good theology, or so that our doctrinal statements are accurate and concise. Statements like this are launching pads into encounters where we experience the very things that are on the page. Jesus here is showing us what is possible to any person that has been cleansed of sin by the blood of Jesus.

THE PRACTICE OF HEALING...

During the days of the Roman Empire, much of what was then called the Church had little understanding or assurance of salvation. While the experience of salvation by faith has always been a part of the true Church, this revelation was put on the back burner for most. But a few hundred years ago, it was moved to the forefront, and the Church began to proclaim again that salvation is only by faith. Even so, it was more of a prolonged process than it is today. Many would seek God in prayer and search the Scriptures, sometimes for weeks or even months, before having the assurance that they had been born again. Many died not knowing the assurance of their salvation. But because the Church embraced this revelation wholeheartedly, teaching it, practicing it, building up people's faith in it, today we consider it the simplest thing in the world. We pray for a sinner to receive Jesus, and we have absolutely no doubt that he or she will be instantly converted. Many of us don't realize that it's only "easy" now because previous generations labored in planting and watering this revelation by putting it into practice. For two centuries the Church in this nation has not lost sight of the power of conversion. It has taught it, preached it, gone into the streets with it, written books about it. Today we are riding the wave of a heritage of faith that has increased for many generations.

A similar thing happened with worship. Over the last hundred years or so, worship has changed significantly. It used to be staid and somber, never personal in its expression to God. Then certain churches and movements began to worship with exuberance, loud voices and raised hands—expressions that most mainstream Christians of the day rejected and ridiculed. Those "extreme worshipers" paid a price. But today you can go into almost any brand of church and see people exalting the name of Jesus with hands and voices raised. Our understanding of this revelation has come through experience and practice, and the church's "mind" has been renewed.

The revelation of healing is on a similar trajectory. Christians are absolutely responsible for bringing divine healing to people, "proving the will of God," bringing earthly reality into line with what's true in heaven. Healing is part of the normal Christian life. God put it in His book; He illustrated it in the life of Jesus. He told us to emulate what Jesus did. So why is it so easy for us to be fully convinced when we pray for someone to be saved that our prayer will work, and yet when we pray for healing we find it difficult to believe they will be healed? Because salvation, as it pertains to a born-again experience, has been embraced and taught continuously by the Church for centuries, while the revelation of healing has not been widely embraced, and has even been fought. Today in many churches, if you pray for people to be healed you are considered to be working under the influence of the devil, while disease is considered a gift from God to make people better Christians! Think about how badly the Church has backslidden, to believe such lies! We have tolerated the deception that accuses God of doing evil, which is why today healing remains so controversial, little-practiced and little-understood.

What would have happened if centuries ago Christians had embraced the power of the gospel to bring healing to the physical body, to the emotions, and to the mind? What if the Church had plowed through that tough soil for generation after generation? Instead of a few "heroes of healing" marking the trail of history, the entire Body of Christ would recognize healing as an essential part of the Great Commission. Normal Christians would see deformities and say, "No problem." Cancer, "No problem." Missing limbs, "No problem." We would pray in power without one iota of doubt.

Can you imagine Jesus telling blind Bartimaeus, "This blindness is a gift from My Father to make you a better person"? And yet that's the approach most Christians take. They don't understand healing because they have no experience with it. They have not put the revelation into practice. I've grown so tired of people praying for blind people and asking God to open the eyes of their heart. The problem is with their natural eyes! The Church doesn't know what to do with blind people, or anyone with a real affliction.

Part of what holds us back is our concern with being excessive. We don't want people to think we're religious nuts; we fear excess much more than we fear lack. So many Christians avoid the subject of healing. You've probably heard a brother or sister in the Lord say, "You should read this book. It's really good, but be careful because the guy has a strange doctrine on such-and-such point." People love to add warnings. But has anyone ever given you a tape or book and said, "This guy's teaching is great, but be careful because he has never raised the dead. Cancer doesn't leave people's bodies when he prays"? No, because as a body we lack experiential understanding of the revelation of healing and the supernatural.

When you put a revelation into practice, you won't get it 100 percent right. You might not even get it 50 percent right. But you will learn, and you will grow into a level of maturity you wouldn't otherwise have. At our church, the only way we know to learn is to experiment. We fail a lot and occasionally we get it right. But we are light years ahead of where we would have been had we not tried at all. I know people today who get excited when they come across somebody who is physically ill or dying. They see crutches, canes, wheelchairs, and casts, and they rejoice. One young man I know walks into a store and sees somebody with a broken leg and thinks, "God loves me so much that He put a man with a broken leg right in front of me." Then he ministers to them and people get healed! His perspective is absolutely reversed. He does not avoid the impossible; he is drawn to it. He is convinced that God is showing him favor by putting somebody in front of him who needs a supernatural intervention.

One pastor and his wife in my area have a passion for healing. They were in a Target parking lot and saw a man with metal crutches, his body twisted up. He was in obvious pain. The pastor's wife, who is passionate about the things of God, asked if she could pray for him and so they took him aside. The man's wife was embarrassed to talk about God and she didn't want anything to do with the impromptu prayer meeting. But this man was miserable, and had been praying for 18 years to die. He allowed them to pray and his body untwisted and became straight. He sprinted around the parking lot, came back, picked up his metal crutches, and threw them across the parking lot. He was absolutely set free and healed.

That's what happens when we unpack our revelation and put it to work in people's lives!

In Rugby, England, a team of us were ministering and there was an elderly man who didn't know he was going deaf, but his neighbors knew because he had his television way too loud. This man finally said, "I need prayer." Somebody prayed for him and he was healed. After he got healed he said, "Oh, this is horrible! Everything is too loud." He had been living in a very quiet world and he enjoyed that!

Another woman we met on that trip to England was rolled out of the back of a station wagon on a cot. She was bedridden because of fibromyalgia. She received prayer from someone on the team, got out of the bed, and walked to the car. They stuck the bed in the back and she rode home in the front seat, for the first time in five years.

One of the most bizarre healings I've seen involved a man who so injured his leg that doctors severed the tendons in his ankles, turned his foot outward for balance and put pins in to lock his ankle. He had no movement, no flex, but he could walk in a limited way. I had a word of knowledge about God healing somebody's left ankle, and this man responded and received prayer from somebody. I don't know exactly what God did, but the man gained full use of his ankle, in spite of the complex mechanisms meant to keep it stationary.

Jesus had one concern about His return and it wasn't that He would find people who were excessive. Rather, He said,

I tell you that He will avenge them speedily. Nevertheless, when the Son of Man comes, will He really find faith on the earth? (Luke 18:8)

When you put your revelation into practice, what used to be impossible will begin to look logical. Your area of faith will expand. That revelation will bring you into an experience and empower you to do the works of the Kingdom.

As we put revelation into practice we gain the opportunity to become students of miracles, rather than just observers. It's critical that we see through the miracle to the lesson God wants us to learn. We'll talk about how to be "tutored" by miracles next.

CHAPTER 5

BECOMING STUDENTS
OF MIRACLES

We must learn to "see" by observing the effect
of the unseen world on all that is visible. Miracles provide
that opportunity more than any other Christian activity.

One Sunday night a young man in our church fell in the
back of the sanctuary and broke his arm. The mother came to
me quickly and said, "Come pray for my son." The healing of
broken bones, even the ones from decades ago that healed in-
correctly, had become commonplace. I ran back and found
him laid out on the ground, his arm clearly broken. I got
down on the ground with him, put my hand on his arm,
looked at the break—and suddenly fear stole into my mind. I
forgot every miracle I had ever seen, and I said, "Let's call the
doctor." Now, I wouldn't fault anyone for calling the doctor in
that circumstance. For most it would be the proper thing to
do. But for me the moment was personally revealing. I had
seen deformed bones disappear, bones re-set, hips reshaped,
blind eyes opened, deaf ears unstopped—but now, looking at
a young man with a broken arm, I forgot everything I had
seen. I switched from supernatural mode to natural mode. My
experience with miracles hadn't fully shaped me. I repented

and apologized to the mother a week or so later, not because I felt guilty or ashamed, but because I realized I had a long way to go in having my mind renewed.

It's not enough to put our revelation into practice, as we saw in the last chapter; we must also become students of miracles. That means the miracles we experience must shape how we think. Miracles can be dazzling and dramatic, but they are not primarily designed to dazzle us. God gives us miracles to train us how to see differently. A miracle is a school. Or think of it this way: Just as there are nutrients in food, so every situation and encounter with God comes filled with the "nutrients" necessary to make us strong as representatives of God on this planet. The problem is that we may go through life experiencing encounters and miracles with God while not extracting what was intended for us in those experiences. We may flunk every test. We may not extract the nutrients. You can see this happen all the time in churches. When God does a miracle, some people say, "Wow, that's really cool," and they leave unchanged. They are thankful, but they have not learned to see differently. They go home and their life continues on in the very same pattern as before, only now they have one more fun thing they got to see God do.

If that has happened to you, don't feel too bad. It happened to Jesus' disciples, too. They participated in a mind-boggling miracle of a great multiplication of food (see Mark 6). The multiplication actually took place in *their* hands, not in Jesus' hands, and that's a key point to remember. Jesus didn't say, "Shazam!" and create a huge pile of food. He didn't wave His hand over the food and watch it increase. He took the small portion they had and divided it into 12 groups, and as the disciples gave it away, it was replenished. But—and here's where they flunked the test—later that day, Jesus told them to cross over to the other side in their boat, and He went to a mountainside to pray. There, He saw in His spirit the disciples straining at rowing, almost ready to lose their lives, so He came walking on the sea close enough to check on them. They saw Him and screamed for fear, and He ended up coming into the boat. The winds and the waves stopped. The disciples settled down. They were completely amazed "For they had not understood about the loaves, because their heart was hardened" (Mark 6:52).

That's an odd ending to that story, but it teaches us this one thing: They had obeyed perfectly when carrying out the miracle of the loaves and fishes, yet their hearts still remained hard. They hadn't *seen through* the miracle. It had not transformed them. You and I can obey God perfectly, and be the instrument that brings about the miracle and still have a hard heart through it and after it. It doesn't mean you're going to hell, but that you missed the lesson of the miracle. The seed of further transformation could not penetrate and take root in your heart.

The disciples did everything Jesus said to do, and yet when they got to the next problem, it came to light that they didn't learn the lesson from the previous one.

What was the lesson? They should have seen their role in the miracle. Because they didn't see their role in the previous miracle, the next time they encountered a problem and Jesus wasn't in the boat, they had no solution. Jesus had said, "*You* give them something to eat." He didn't say, "I'll do it for you." It was at their touch, their obedience, that the food multiplied. And yet they missed the whole point.

Jesus' goal wasn't to send them into a storm so He could show up and be the hero. He planned to pass by, but they weren't understanding the lesson. They did not extract the nutrients from the last miracle. That hardness of heart prevented them from becoming deliverers, and so Jesus had to deliver them once again.

THE LEAVENS OF THE MIND...

The Bible talks about influences on the mind that determine how we interact with the Kingdom. These influences affect us as we endeavor to become students of miracles. Jesus put it this way in Matthew 13:33:

> *Another parable He spoke to them: "The kingdom of heaven is like leaven, which a woman took and hid in three measures of meal till it was all leavened."*

Jesus spoke again of leaven in Mark 8:13-21:

> *And He left them, and getting into the boat again, departed to the other side. Now the disciples had forgotten to take bread, and they did not have more than one loaf with them in the boat. Then He charged them, saying, "Take heed, beware of the leaven of the Pharisees and the leaven of Herod." And they reasoned among themselves, saying, "It is because we have no bread." But Jesus, being aware of it, said to them, "Why do you reason because you have no bread? Do you not yet perceive nor understand? Is your heart still hardened? Having eyes, do you not see? And having ears, do you not hear? And do you not remember? When I broke the five loaves for the five thousand, how many baskets full of fragments did you take up?" They said to Him, "Twelve." "Also, when I broke the seven for the four thousand, how many large baskets full of fragments did you take up?" And they said, "Seven." So He said to them, "How is it you do not understand?"*

In saying, "Be careful of the leaven of the Pharisees and the leaven of Herod," He was warning them about influences on the mind that can rob us of the nutrients of revelation and renewal. Three kinds of leavens are mentioned in the above verses: the leaven of Herod, the Pharisees, and the Kingdom. These leavens are alive and active today and they greatly affect how you think, how you live, and everything about your life.

Leaven is a picture of influence on our minds. Leaven in the natural realm causes dough to rise. My wife used to make bread, and if the bread wasn't rising, we would set it by the wood stove, and the heat would activate the leaven. The fire of difficulty similarly causes the leaven in your life to be exposed and brought to the surface. If your mind is permeated by Kingdom leaven as Jesus talked about in Matthew 13, then the Kingdom reality of faith will come to the surface. If it is the leaven of Herod or the leaven of the Pharisees, it disrupts revelation and Kingdom work.

Let's look at each of these in a little more depth.

HEROD'S LEAVEN...

The leaven of Herod is an atheistic influence based on the strength of man and man-based systems, like politics, popular will, and persuasion. Herod's leaven excludes God entirely. Its statement of faith is a cynical, "God helps those who help themselves." If you found yourself in the boat without bread, the person under this influence would advise, "Next time write a list and remember to bring bread. You are the answer to your own problem. Take responsibility for yourself. Be a self-made person."

Herod's leaven represents one of the big problems in the Church: practical atheism. Large numbers of Christians are practical atheists who disbelieve in an active God. They wouldn't say it that way; no church's written doctrine would declare there is no God. But believers face situations daily without bringing God into the picture. Like Herod, they say there is no divine intervention in practical living. They are professing

Christians but live exactly like their atheist neighbors whenever they face a problem. They don't think to get God's counsel through His Word, or invite God to intervene.

American culture is permeated with the leaven of Herod. We're a country of self-made people, pioneers who think that through determination, discipline, and administrative excellence we can accomplish whatever we want. Sometimes the Church falls into the deception of thinking that whatever we can accomplish in our own strength has been directed or honored by God. But many things the Church has done in the last hundred years, God had nothing to do with. We have money, we have unity of heart and mind, and we have some administrative skills to accomplish our goals. But it doesn't mean they were born in the heart of God. They may have been born of our desire to accomplish something great, whether or not God was involved in our efforts.

PHARISEE LEAVEN...

The leaven of the Pharisees is different from Herod's. Pharisee leaven represents the religious system. It embraces God in theory, but not in practice or experience. The concept of God is essential to the Pharisaical mind, but the experience of God is completely removed. The Pharisees have God in form but without power. If you found yourself without bread in the boat with a Pharisee, he would say, "God in His sovereignty has arranged for you to be in this boat without any bread so that you could better identify with those who also have no bread in this hour." Pharisees provides explanations, not solutions. They say the bakery closed when the last apostle died. They refuse to let God be active right now on earth. They insist that you pray, but also insist you should have no hope of God answering. Theirs is a Russian roulette God: spin the chamber and maybe you'll get an answer...or maybe not.

People under the influence of Pharisee leaven can know Jesus the wrong way, like the people of Nazareth did. They knew Jesus in form, but not in relationship or demonstration (see Mark 6). Today, countless millions in the Church have been satisfied with Pharisee leaven. They are content with some documentation that they belong to a certain brand of church, but they are entirely unplugged from an active, invasive, here-and-now God.

Under the influence of this leaven, many Christians find explanations for physical illnesses that do not bring the power of God into the picture. They say, "That person is tormented by that particular affliction, but with the lifestyle he leads, it's no wonder." They feel a cocky sense of understanding at explaining the problem, and yet they are powerless to provide a solution, and they vilify anyone who tries. The disciples fell into this, too. They asked Jesus, "Rabbi, who sinned, this man or his parents, that he was born blind?" (John 9:2) Jesus refused to discuss that question with them. He said, "Neither this man nor his parents sinned, but that the works of God should be revealed in him" (John 9:3). People just don't realize that when God redeems a situation He does it so thoroughly that it looks like He created the problem as an opportunity for His power or glory to be seen. The same could be said of sin. Yet God did not make a person sin just so His glory could be revealed. When Jesus is at hand, a problem takes on purpose. Without His redemptive touch, the problem is just another work of the devil. Jesus was so focused on solutions that He didn't even entertain the Pharisaical debate.

Jesus exposed the core characteristic of the influences of Herod and the Pharisees: both are based on the fear of man. Both are primarily motivated by what people think. But when we are influenced by Kingdom leaven, we don't fear what people think about us. God is raising up a people who are considerate, compassionate, and caring, but who are also not motivated one bit by a fear of man. Instead they live out of the fear of God. Psalm 25:14 says,

> The secret of the Lord is with those who fear Him, and He will show them His covenant.

Proverbs 29:25 says,

> The fear of man brings a snare, but whoever trusts in the Lord shall be safe.

The fear of God makes our sight clear. The fear of man makes us endlessly confused.

THE LEAVEN OF THE KINGDOM...

Jesus warned against Herod's and the Pharisees' leavens because they work against the renewal of our minds. In the immediate context when Jesus spoke these words, the great failure of the disciples was that they were afraid because they didn't pack a lunch, and Jesus had multiplied food for them twice. Their thought life began with what they lacked, and so they contradicted the revelation God had just given them about supernatural provision. They built their thought life on the improper foundation. In the previous chapter of Mark, Jesus said to another set of people, "Thus you have made the commandment of God of no effect by your tradition" (Matt. 15:6). That's what happened to the disciples. The plug gets pulled on God's power whenever we resort to tradition rather than the continual, fresh hearing of the Word of God. Tradition isn't necessarily an evil thing; it's just usually yesterday's word. The Bible says faith comes from hearing—not from having heard.

The disciples had that fresh word, but they didn't get it. "Why do you reason because you have no bread?" Jesus said. "Do you not yet perceive nor understand? Is your heart still hardened?" (Mark 8:17) He did not talk to them this way before they fed the multitudes, because they had no reference point. They did not know by experience what God could do. But God led them into the experience expecting them to make that miracle the new standard for their lives.

When God does a miracle for you, and you get to see it and be a part of it, He is teaching you how to see into the invisible realm. A miracle is a tutor, a gift from God to show us what exists on the other side. When I experience a miracle, and later revert back to the same doubt, complaining, moaning, and groaning, it's because I have not allowed the testimony of the Lord to have its full effect on the way I think. When I saw that boy's broken arm, my mind was flooded with fear instead of being flooded with the testimony of miracles I'd seen with my own eyes. It may have looked like wisdom to everybody else when I called the doctor, but God knew and I knew it was fear. Sometimes fear masquerades as wisdom. I had to lose consciousness, if you will—lose my awareness of my history with seeing miracles.

You and I can be the most Kingdom-minded people on the planet when things are going well. We can see dozens healed, dozens saved, have great times of worship. But then I might go home and the car breaks down and suddenly I'm out $3,000. Then the computer shuts off and the phone system goes out, and the neighbor's mad at me. The fire of circumstance expands whatever leaven is influencing my mind. Malachi 3:2 says, "For He is like a refiner's fire." Malachi 4:1 says,

For behold, the day is coming, burning like an oven.

He is talking about a series of events that will draw certain influences to the surface where we can plainly see them—whether we like them or not.

99

I wish my first response to adversity was always to have faith. Sometimes it takes me a day or two, sometimes only a few minutes to get my heart and mind right. There are times when I get so troubled, so provoked and anxious, and I know biblically there is no reason for it. I always wonder, how can I be so worried and bogged down by pressures when He bought me with a price, gave me His Son, and will freely give me all things? Only because the leaven of Herod or the Pharisees has worked its way into my soul, and the pressure caused the leaven to rise.

Kingdom thinking knows that anything is possible at any time. It's activated when you and I with tender hearts surrender to the thought patterns of God, when we receive His imaginations and say "yes." We want our minds to be full of Kingdom leaven, Kingdom influence. We want miracles, and we want those miracles to have their full effect on us, changing the way we see and behave.

WHERE DID YOUR STORM COME FROM...

The storms of life, like miracles, can present terrific challenges and opportunities for us to grow. But it makes a great deal of difference which kind of storm you're in. Some storms, though sent by the devil, can provoke us and invite us to use the revelation we already have. They are miracles waiting to happen, as in this passage from Mark 4:35-41:

> On the same day, when evening had come, He said to them, "Let us cross over to the other side." Now when they had left the multitude, they took Him along in the boat as He was. And other little boats were also with Him. And a great windstorm arose, and the waves beat into the boat, so that it was already filling. But He was in the stern, asleep on a pillow. And they awoke Him and said to Him, "Teacher, do You not care that we are perishing?" Then He arose and

rebuked the wind, and said to the sea, "Peace, be still!" And the wind ceased and there was a great calm. But He said to them, "Why are you so fearful? How is it that you have no faith?" And they feared exceedingly, and said to one another, "Who can this be, that even the wind and the sea obey Him!"

But there are other kinds of storms God sends to show us we're going in the wrong direction, like this familiar one:

But the Lord sent out a great wind on the sea, and there was a mighty tempest on the sea, so that the ship was about to be broken up. Then the mariners were afraid; and every man cried out to his god, and threw the cargo that was in the ship into the sea, to lighten the load. But Jonah had gone down into the lowest parts of the ship, had lain down, and was fast asleep. So the captain came to him, and said to him, "What do you mean, sleeper? Arise, call on your God; perhaps your God will consider us, so that we may not perish" (Jonah 1:4-6).

We see in these passages two storms, and two different purposes for each storm. One was sent by God, the other by the devil. Each situation involved a man sleeping in the boat, one because of depression and a way of escaping his unpleasant reality, the other because He was living from the Kingdom toward earth, and in the Kingdom there was no storm.

The question is, which storm are you in? And are you dealing with it the way God wants you to deal with it? Have you let past miracles "tutor" you to a place of faith adequate for your current challenge?

The disciples' storm was sent by the devil to keep them from the will of God. Jonah's storm was sent by God to turn him back to the will of God. Some people face storms because they took a left when God took a right. God brings a storm in

His mercy to drive them back. Others face storms *because they are in the middle of God's will.* He doesn't like the storm, but He wants to train you to use tools He's given you to calm the storm.

Most of us find ourselves in a storm and instantly conclude our job is to cry out to God to intervene and change our circumstance. But that's not the purpose of the storm; if we only cry out, we are abdicating our role in a miracle. God never allows a storm without first providing the tools to calm the storm. He wants us to use those tools to bring about a miraculous result. Think of the greatest conflict or crisis in your life in the last year. I assure you, with some examination, you can identify the tools God put in your life to take care of that problem. He allows problems into our lives so we can defeat them—not only so we can cry out to Him every time. The tools will be in the boat with us, but the enemy will fan the winds of fear to get us to forget where the tools are.

So many of us see the storm and pray what the disciples prayed when they saw Jesus sleeping in the boat: "Don't You care that we're perishing?" Jesus got up and answered their prayer. Most of us feel good when God answers our prayers. We might even applaud the disciples for doing the right thing in this circumstance, but Jesus turned to them and said, "How come you don't have any faith?" "Wait a minute!" they might have thought. "I had enough faith to come and to talk to You! And You did what I asked! I thought I was paid to pray, and you were paid to do!" No, it is our responsibility to command that obstacle to disappear. Most people's ministry involves trying to get God to fix problems on earth when we should be commanding the storms to be calm. We should see situations from heaven's perspective and declare the word of the Lord—and watch heaven invade.

I have tremendous love and respect for the ministry of intercession, as I'm married to a great intercessor. But many intercessors moan and groan and weep and are depressed all of the time and call that intercession. They never come into a place of faith when they pray. I know what that's like. There have been seasons in my life when I prayed great lengths of time, very diligently, very disciplined, very impressive if I were to have counted the hours. God never penalized me for it because He knew the sincerity of my heart. But in reality, of the time I spent praying, very little of it was in faith. Most of it was in depression, discouragement or "burden."

The tragedy is that many believers can't yet distinguish the difference between the burden of the Lord and the weight of their own unbelief.

The worse some people feel when they're through praying, the more they feel gratified to be an anointed intercessor. It's okay to start there, but do whatever is necessary to arrive at a place of faith.

That kind of wayward intercession is the opposite of what Jesus expects of us when we face storms. If Jesus is sleeping in your boat, it's not because He's waiting for you to wake Him up with your wailing or earnest prayers. It's because you have divine purpose. He's wanting you to use the tools He has given you to bring about the "heavenly" result. Some teachers teach that God likes to wait until the last minute to intervene and show His sovereignty. They think that's His cute and clever way of showing He was in control the whole time. You hear people say, "God's never early or late, but He's always right on time." But God doesn't always work that way. If He always intervenes at the last minute, it's often because we didn't use the tools we'd been given in the first place!

If you are facing a spiritual battle, it is usually because you have been trained for that moment. It means you have experienced things in your life that should have taught you how to respond to the present storm. When problems come, you should already know the right thing to do. You shouldn't have to seek God in hours of discouraged prayer. You should be ready to step in and say, "I believe God for a miracle in this situation. That backslidden child will return home. That disease in your body is broken in the name of Jesus. That financial crisis is over." The time to pray is beforehand, like Jesus did, crying out to God in private times when nothing was going wrong. That's how to store up power and create an inner atmosphere of peace and faith that you take with you into the troubling situation.

Let's not waste our miracles. Let's not watch God do something awesome, then give a little golf clap, a little "amen" and walk away unchanged. Let's recognize that we are equipped for each storm. We have been trained by past miracles to see present solutions. Let's allow the leaven of the Kingdom to fill our minds, replacing the leaven of Herod and of the Pharisees. Let's allow our revelation and experience of God to forever change the way we approach this life.

In the next section, we'll look at the most common hindrances that get in the way of our minds being renewed, and keep us from fully living the normal Christian life. Then we'll see how to overcome them!

CHAPTER 6

GUILT-FREE AND FORGIVEN

*Jesus got what I deserved so that
I could get what He deserved.*

We have seen that the point of our lives is out of a place of intimacy to do God's will on earth as it is in heaven. We have seen how our minds are the gatekeepers of the miraculous and must be renewed if we are to see reality from God's perspective. We have seen how revelation must be put into action, and that miracles are tutors and opportunities to change the way we live from that point on.

Now I want to pause and talk about the common obstacles people come up against as they seek to live in the supernatural and renew their minds. I heard a story of a European family who wanted to move to the United States, so they worked hard and saved enough money to take a ship across the Atlantic. They also saved as much as they could to buy cheese and crackers, provisions they could eat as a family in the small ship's cabin they would occupy. They boarded the ship and days and weeks went by. The family huddled in their cabin eating their meager provisions, all while listening to the footsteps and laughter of people in the hallway on their way to eat in the banquet room. On the last night of their long sea journey the captain announced they would make landfall in

the United States the next day. The father decided to cele-
brate by taking the family to the banquet room where everyone else on the ship had been eating for three weeks. He
approached the captain and asked how much the meal cost.
The captain looked at him in surprise and said, "You mean
you haven't been eating there? Those meals were included in
the price of the fare."

I strongly believe that many Christians eat cheese and
crackers, in spiritual terms, when our "fare" bought us a full
banquet. I'm not talking about financial wealth, although
God destroyed the power of poverty at the Cross. I'm talking
about salvation and the forgiveness of sin. Too often Christians live under the influence of yesterday's failures, blemish-
es, and mistakes. When we do, we depart from the normal
Christian lifestyle and live under the influence of a lie. Need-
less to say, this lie halts the renewing of our minds and keeps
us from living in the "everyday miraculous" that should be
normal for every born-again believer.

Why do people receive God's forgiveness but constantly
live under the shadow of their failures? I know from personal
experience that I used to willingly live under the guilt and
shame of bad decisions from yesterday because I thought it
helped me walk in humility. I would get down in the mouth
and dwell on my shortcomings. I never was good at talking
about it with friends. Instead, I internalized it. But as I focused
on my character problems, they grew overwhelmingly large. I
fed them with an unrenewed mind, and the power of agreement came upon the problem and multiplied its apparent
size. The damage done in my own emotions and thought life
was horrendous.

Other people similarly resist forgiveness because they
don't want to be prideful. Remembering how rotten they are
makes them feel good, but it's actually a subtle form of pride.

People moan and groan, "I'm not worthy." Of course we're not worthy! It's time we get over it and live the Christian life anyway. Living under yesterday's condemnation doesn't make us more humble. If anything, it keeps us focused on ourselves instead of on the Lord. It's much more difficult to humbly receive forgiveness we don't deserve than to walk in false humility, cloaked in yesterday's shame. When we receive free forgiveness, the one who gave it to us is honored. When He is honored, we are truly humbled.

When we succumb to guilt and shame, we give in to the single oldest temptation in the Bible: the temptation to question our identity and God's identity. The very first temptation in the Bible was not to partake of forbidden fruit, but to question what God had said. The serpent said, "Has God indeed said, 'You shall not eat of every tree of the garden'?" (Gen. 3:1b). Once he got them to doubt God's integrity and identity, it was easy to lure them into foolish actions. In the same way, before the devil tempted Jesus with anything else, he tried to pry Him away from His identity: "*If* You are the Son of God..." (Matt. 4:6). He wanted Jesus to doubt His identity— so what is the devil's strategy with you and me? The same thing!

Probably 95 percent or more of all counseling that churches undertake is simply to help people stop questioning what God has said and to stop questioning who we are in Christ. We are the people God loves, the people God forgives. We are the House of God, the gate of heaven on earth. When Moses asked God, "Who am I that I should go to Pharaoh, and that I should bring the children of Israel out of Egypt?" (Gen. 3:11), God appeared to ignore the question by answering, "I will certainly be with you" (Gen. 3:12). But that was the answer! Moses said, "Who am I?" God said, in effect, "You are the man God goes with." Who are you, brother or sister? You are the person that God hangs around with. You are clean and forgiven. That is your identity!

You've Been Bought...

God is never honored when we deny what Jesus did for us. He suffered so we would be free. What parent delights in seeing his or her child suffer? Neither does God delight in seeing us suffer with the effects of guilt and shame. Yet we often ascribe that evil motive to the Father.

This may come as a shock to you, but when Jesus bought you, He bought your problem! I've seen the fruit of my own stupid mistakes wiped out completely on some occasions; God paid the bill and let me off the hook. On other occasions, I've had to live with the fruit of those mistakes, facing them every month when the bill came. But even then I faced them not as my problem to fix, but His problem. You see, justice takes on a different perspective once you are washed in the blood of Jesus.

Isaiah 61:1 says the prison would be opened for those who were bound. In truth, prisoners are usually in prison because they did something wrong. How does biblical justice set a prisoner free when there is a price to pay? It depends on your definition of "justice." Once you come to Jesus and repent of what you did, He aims for true justice, which addresses not you but the power that influenced you. That's huge. Maybe you cheated on your taxes, or wrongly criticized a friend, or did something more horrible than that. When you truly repent and are forgiven, you become a partner with the Lord in addressing it. You do everything possible to make restitution, but there is no longer any guilt and shame. Now His justice is aimed at the powers of hell that deceived you into acting on greed, or anger, or whatever it was. You now are in a place to inspire people to walk uprightly in that area. Why? Because you got bit once, and the memory is real.

I'll say it again: When Jesus bought you, He bought your problem. That's liberating! The Bible tells us to "Likewise...

reckon yourselves to be dead indeed to sin, but alive to God in Christ Jesus our Lord" (Rom. 6:11). That word *likewise* means "evaluate, take an account of, do the math and come to a conclusion." We either believe that His provision was adequate or we don't. Unfortunately, many believers constantly battle a phantom self-image from the past with no assurance of their present identity in Christ. Forgiveness seems like a theory or an impractical truth. Yet it is the most practical truth there is.

Paul insisted we keep this in mind. In Romans 6, he illustrated the nature of the Christian life through water baptism, concluding in verse 11, "reckon yourselves to be dead indeed to sin." Are you washed in the blood of Jesus? Then you need to think of yourself as dead to sin. It's not a mind-over-matter thing, but has everything to do with the power of supernatural thinking. It's waking up to what's been real and true since the moment you met Jesus: *As a born-again follower of Christ, you are dead to sin.* Paul wrote,

> *How shall we who died to sin live any longer in it? Or do you not know that as many of us as were baptized into Christ Jesus were baptized into His death? Therefore we were buried with Him through baptism into death, that just as Christ was raised from the dead by the glory of the Father, even so we also should walk in newness of life. For if we have been united together in the likeness of His death, certainly we also shall be in the likeness of His resurrection, knowing this, that our old man was crucified with Him, that the body of sin might be done away with, that we should no longer be slaves of sin. For he who has died has been freed from sin. Now if we died with Christ, we believe that we shall also live with Him, knowing that Christ, having been raised from the dead, dies no more. Death no longer has dominion over Him. For the death that He died,*

He died to sin once for all; but the life that He lives, He lives to God (Romans 6:2b-10).

The death of Christ wiped out our record of sin. This may seem like grammar school teaching, but most people don't live with the realization that they are totally forgiven. They can quote the passage, but they don't live under the influence of its truth. The blood of Jesus wiped out the power and record of sin in your life. Your old nature is dead. It hasn't been put on a shelf, or in a closed room, or imprisoned—it has been crucified. Period. Done deal.

Remember that Jesus addressed believers as saints. We tend to think sainthood is acquired after years of sacrificial service. Wrong. We went from rotten sinners to born-again saints in a single moment when we accepted salvation. Once the blood of Jesus has wiped out sin, you can't get any cleaner. That doesn't mean we can avoid the hurdles and issues that come with changing your life and renewing your mind. Maturity is a process. But as my associate Kris says, "You are not a sinner; you are a saint. It doesn't mean that you can't sin; it just means that you are no longer a professional." That's the story of your life.

RENEWED AND FORGIVEN...

It's difficult if not impossible to demonstrate the will of God "on earth as in heaven" if we don't think of ourselves as truly forgiven, and if we hang onto a false view of our identity. It effectively cancels out most of our potential in ministry. Some people reduce each day to, "I hope I survive" instead of, "What will God do today through me?" You and I were designed to triumphantly demonstrate the reality of the King and His Kingdom, but many of us strip our goal down to survival. "If I can get through the day without being depressed, without being discouraged, I will have succeeded," we tell ourselves.

Our first thought of each day should instead be the reality of the Kingdom: "His mercies are new for me every morning!" (Lam. 3:23). Friend, you are forgiven! There's nothing anybody can do to change that. When the enemy brings up a sin from your past, he is talking about something non-existent. It's completely legal for you to say, "I didn't do that. The person who did that is dead. This person has never done that." Either the blood of Jesus is completely effective, or it's not effective at all. And it does not just wipe away the punishment so that when you die you don't go to hell; rather, the blood of Jesus has the power to completely transform us into a new creation in Christ. Romans 8:38-39 says,

> *For I am persuaded that neither death nor life, nor angels nor principalities nor powers, nor things present nor things to come, nor height nor depth, nor any other created thing, shall be able to separate us from the love of God which is in Christ Jesus our Lord.*

There is no power, no circumstance, no person, no demonic reality, no strategy of the devil, nothing in existence right now in heaven or on earth that can separate you from the love of God. But notice that although Paul mentions the present and the future, he doesn't mention the past, because the past *can* separate you from *your awareness* of the love of God, if you let it become your present identity. Remember, Jesus bought your sin, not to bring it up again but to destroy it so you don't have to think about it anymore.

I finally figured out after all these years that the secret to always being encouraged is to live in denial. The enemy puts a request across my desk and I stamp "request denied" on it. He tells me I'm one thing; I deny that assertion and rest in my true identity in Christ. The Bible says that if I walk in the light as He is in the light, I have fellowship with Him, and the outcome is that the blood of Jesus continuously washes me clean (see 1 John 1:7). If I am open and honest and stay right in my relationships with God and with people, the blood of Jesus keeps me clean 24 hours a day, non-stop.

Thinking of ourselves as rotten sinners, always recalling the bad thing we did sometime in our past, robs us of a renewed mind and keeps us from stepping into the supernatural, normal life. God is never honored when we recall and live under the influence of our sins and blunders of yesterday. Many people grow older and live with so much regret. I could go back to that way of thinking really quickly, but I know better now. I know the right way is to embrace your forgiven-ness. Insist on your identity in Him. Let your heart be light with the realization that His mercies are new *for you* each morning. You'll not only be happier, you'll be much more effective for the Kingdom.

You might dwell on this for a while and let it saturate your understanding. Live in this truth and let it multiply in your life over the next few days and weeks. You'll see a major difference when you start living free and forgiven, with no baggage to haul around. In the next chapter we discuss remembering as a way of renewing our minds.

Chapter 7

Remembering

The Promises of God are like the rudder to a ship.
Reviewing them sets the direction for my whole life.

An associate of mine, Mike, and I were in the airport in Vancouver, Canada, waiting in line at Starbucks (one of my favorite places). As I stood there enjoying the aromas, the sights and sounds of the coffee shop, and the anticipation of my next cup of coffee, I noticed Mike was taking a long time with the cashier. It didn't occur to me that anything important was happening. I was simply there getting coffee as we waited for our next flight. Then I saw him take the cashier's hand, and they closed their eyes and bowed their heads in prayer. When they had finished, Mike joined me and told me that as he was ordering, he had seen a spirit of suicide on her, and he began to minister to her and broke that power. She told him, "God sent you in here today." I was caught off guard because all I was thinking about was coffee! My mind had momentarily forgotten the more important things in life.

It's easy for our minds to stray into natural thinking only, for our faith to erode so subtly that we don't notice it happening. Little by little we can begin to think "practically," leaning on natural wisdom instead of Kingdom reality. One of the great tools for keeping a Kingdom mindset is to meditate on and remember God's Word, devising ways of reminding ourselves of His promises to us, and then passing those promises and remembrances on to the next generation of believers. Without taking practical steps to remember and meditate on the truth, we will easily forget what God has promised. By degrees, we will become earthly minded, and that's what we must avoid if we're to successfully live the normal Christian life.

MEDITATION DONE RIGHT...

In Eastern occult religions, meditation means emptying the mind. But biblical meditation is the opposite—it's filling the mind with God's truth. Some Christians don't like the idea of meditation because they've only seen it demonstrated in a corrupt way through diabolical religions. But if you've ever worried about something, you already know how to meditate! Every person, saint and sinner alike, meditates every day. The question is, what are you meditating on? Say you've got a problem with your finances. A person with a renewed mind derives joy even in that circumstance because joy comes not by what is seen but by what God says. God is not a liar and He will keep His word. But a little voice called worry steals in and reasons with you, saying, "Years ago you disobeyed the Lord financially, and now you will reap what you sowed." That might sound like a pretty good argument, and it might cause you to shift your meditation from God's Word to worry. Soon that little voice has grown so big it's like a megaphone in your ear. You forget that God said He would "keep him in perfect peace, whose mind is stayed on" Him (Isa. 26:3). Perfect peace means divine health, prosperity, wellness of being, soundness of mind. *Stayed* or *fixed* means "braced, lodged in an immovable position." But when we listen to worry, we become "unfixed." Why does worry shout so loudly for our attention? Because if we look at it long enough, it will gain our trust. Pretty soon we begin praying out of fear, and eventually we quit praying and start looking for sympathy. We have trusted that other voice, and it won the affections of our heart.

We must get our minds set on spiritual things because as long as we fill our minds with what's happening in the natural, we restrict our effectiveness. We may rise up now and then and score a victory with the gift of faith, but we won't have the continual influence of Kingdom transformation flowing through us.

What's the solution? To meditate on the Word and give ourselves every opportunity to remember what is true. The Bible speaks clearly about how to do this:

WRITE IT DOWN...

Habakkuk 2:2 says,

Write the vision and make it plain on tablets, that he may run who reads it.

People need motivation to run. That's the main reason I travel and speak and write as much as I can. I want to give other people the fuel they need to get up and go. I want them to have whatever revelation I have, just as I feed on the revelation given to me by others. To participate in the active, awesome work of the Kingdom we can't casually row, row, row our boat gently down the stream. We've got to run!

That's why I do as Habakkuk advised and write down God's ideas about my life whenever they are revealed to me. I mark up and underline my Bible every which way. I write down prophecies I've received on note cards and in my computer, and I carry those with me wherever I go. I post Post-It notes on the dashboard of my car. I put them all over the church sometimes so that when I walk around and pray I see cards everywhere, reminding me of what God is saying. I keep a journal for my children and my grandchildren that they might see what God did in my lifetime. We even have a staff member at our church whose entire job description is to record the miracles that happen in and through our church and with our ministry teams. I want people to know the great and mighty works of the Lord long after we're gone, so they can run with the vision even further.

REVIEW IT...

Of course, a written record is only useful when you review it. *Re* means "to go back," and view means "to see." *Go back* over God's promises until *you can see!* Sometimes I need to re-visit those prophetic words that were spoken over me, so I go through the stack of cards and read the ones I need. They are the facts of my life, because God spoke them. It's not simply positive thinking or using my imagination to trick myself into believing some alternate reality. It's meditating on what God has said until I can see it and run with it.

At other times I will sit down with people and say, "Remind me what happened in such-and-such city when we ministered there. Tell me the story again." The person will say, "Oh, man, that guy with no hip joint got up and walked. And the deaf lady heard for the first time. That broken bone was healed. Remember?" Those conversations remind me of things I have forgotten and reestablish the cornerstones of my thought life. I force my imaginations to become Kingdom imaginations. The testimony of what the Lord has done helps us to remember who God is, what His covenant is like and who He intends to be in our lives. Every testimony of His work in someone's life is a prophecy for those with ears to hear. It is a promise that He'll do the same for us because *God is no respecter of persons* (see Acts 10:34) and *He is the same yesterday, today and forever* (see Heb. 13:8). But the testimony must be heard, spoken, written down, and reviewed. Israel fell into great backsliding when they forgot the testimony (the spoken or written record of what God has done). But when they recalled the testimony of what God did before, anticipation increased, and so did the miracles.

REMIND GOD...

Malachi 3:16 tells us about God's journal:

Then those who feared the Lord spoke to one another, and the Lord listened and heard them; so a book of remembrance was written before Him for those who fear the Lord and who meditate on His name.

Sometimes God reviews what is written in His book of remembrance, and He shapes the future because of what was done in the past. It happened with Cornelius in the Book of Acts:

He and all his family were devout and God-fearing; he gave generously to those in need and prayed to God regularly. One day at about three in the afternoon he had a vision. He distinctly saw an angel of God, who came to him and said, "Cornelius!" Cornelius stared at him in fear. "What is it, Lord?" he asked. The angel answered, "Your prayers and gifts to the poor have come up as a memorial offering before God" (Acts 10:2-5).

That's a wonderful promise that our gifts and work for the Lord are never forgotten or overlooked. But at other times, God instructs us to actively remind Him of what we've done. He invites us to engage Him in this way and to review the circumstances of our lives before Him so that through this interaction we are transformed. When Israel crossed the River Jordan, the leaders of the tribes each took a stone and made a pile on the Promised Land side of the river (see Josh. 4).

The stones were to trigger their memories about what God had done. But they also served to remind God of their condition, their need, and their obedience. Memorial stones that we put before God—in the form of prayer and generosity—remind Him of our condition, our need, and our obedience. Is it possible that God has chosen not to know certain things so that He could discover them in His relationship with us? He gives us a stunning privilege of putting before Him stones of remembrance to remind Him of our past faithfulness.

We see this throughout Scripture. Nehemiah, governor of Jerusalem, helped to rebuild the city. And he laid his case before the Lord,

> *Indeed, I also continued the work on this wall, and we did not buy any land. All my servants were gathered there for the work. And at my table were one hundred and fifty Jews and rulers, besides those who came to us from the nations around us. Now that which was prepared daily was one ox and six choice sheep. Also fowl were prepared for me, and once every ten days an abundance of all kinds of wine. Yet in spite of this I did not demand the governor's provisions, because the bondage was heavy on this people* (Nehemiah 5:16-18).

He concluded:

> *Remember me, my God, for good, according to all that I have done for this people* (Nehemiah 5:19).

He was reminding God, putting a memorial stone before Him.

I'd be interested to know what is written in heaven's book of remembrance, but I think the record of Scripture gives us a good idea. Take the example of Sarah, Abraham's wife. In Genesis 18, she,

Laughed within herself, saying, "After I have grown old, shall I have pleasure, my lord being old also?" And the Lord said to Abraham, "Why did Sarah laugh, saying, 'Shall I surely bear a child, since I am old?' Is anything too hard for the Lord? At the appointed time I will return to you, according to the time of life, and Sarah shall have a son." But Sarah denied it, saying, "I did not laugh," for she was afraid. And He said, "No, but you did laugh!" (Genesis 18:12-15)

She didn't just give an embarrassed giggle. The Hebrew word for *laugh* tells us she was *mocking* what God had said. Not only that, she lied about it when God confronted her. But Hebrews 11:11 says of this same woman,

By faith Sarah herself also received strength to conceive seed, and she bore a child when she was past the age, because she judged Him faithful who had promised.

Wow! The record sure sounds different than the reality! This tells us something precious: the book of remembrance doesn't have a record of our mistakes. Genesis 18 was recorded for human benefit, so you and I could identify with those who followed God in the past. But Hebrews 11 is how it's recorded in the book of remembrance. Once the blood has been applied, there is no record of sin anymore. God brags all over heaven about Sarah, and He does the same about you and me. Maybe you had a bad week, but you stirred yourself to worship God anyway. That was recorded in the book of remembrance. You may have yelled at the kids all the way to church, but when you apologized and sincerely worshiped God and sought His presence, the angels recorded, "So-and-so moved in great faith on this date. She rose above difficult circumstances and saw the purposes of God that were superior to everything in her life." What looked in the natural like an awful Sunday morning was recorded as a great act of faith!

Renewing the mind becomes possible when we remember, record, review, and remind ourselves and God of what He has done in the past, and of our obedience. It is a sure way to solidify your identity in Him, and to mold your mind so it conforms to the mind of Christ.

Next we'll tackle the tough problem of keeping our minds on heaven's reality during times of personal crisis.

CHAPTER 8

ENDURING UNCERTAINTY

I will gladly live in the midst of an unexplainable mystery
before believing a lie to feel better about my circumstances.

One of the toughest lessons a Christian can learn is how to trust and praise God in the uncertain time between a promise and its fulfillment. I believe it is a powerful act of spiritual warfare to stand in the middle of death and disease, conflict and unresolved issues, and to cause your spirit to rise and give thanks to God.

I can't help but think of the experience of one of our most respected missionaries, Tracey. Recently she was driving from South Africa to Mozambique when the small bus just ahead of her went out of control, rolled off the road, and crashed at a speed of about 60 miles per hour. Passengers were thrown from the vehicle as it rolled. She and other motorists stopped to assist and discovered a gruesome scene as they went victim to victim. Many people had life-threatening injuries, traumatic head injuries, and were laying unconscious. One woman was clearly dead. She had no vital signs, her head was facing her back, and she had one eye lying on her cheek. Our missionary, a graduate from Stanford as a Physician's Assistant, took the bystanders and placed them by each of the injured persons. She then instructed them to

"Speak life in Jesus' name. When I look over at you, I want to see your lips moving!" And move, they did!

Minutes later, as she was assessing the casualties, the woman assigned to the dead passenger screamed. The "dead" woman had groaned, turned her head around, and begun to breathe again. To their amazement the woman's vital signs were strong, and her misplaced eye was back in its socket. That caused the others to pray all the more earnestly for their patients. Within a short period of time the unconscious victims had regained consciousness and those with serious wounds stopped bleeding. Many injuries were healed, and people were spared who surely should have died.

When I heard that story, my mind kept coming back to the people who stood by and prayed even when the situation seemed hopeless. That's the kind of attitude we must have during times of uncertainty. Our troubling circumstance may last days, months, or years, instead of just an hour or two, but our approach should be the same: We must declare the goodness and faithfulness of God even in the midst of our trial, before we have an answer.

Why do we have to endure uncertainty? That is a mystery, but the Bible hints at an answer when it gives a spiritual picture of a city called the community of the redeemed, or Zion (see Isa. 62). Isaiah 60:18 says, "But you shall call your walls Salvation, and your gates Praise." In Revelation we see this gate called praise again and discover that is made out of one solid pearl (see Rev. 21:21). Think for a moment. How is a pearl formed? Through irritation and conflict. A granule of sand gets inside an oyster shell, and a pearl forms around the granule to keep it from doing harm. The Bible's pairing of praise with irritation is not coincidental. When we are stuck in conflict and uncertainty, and yet we praise Him without manipulation, it is a sacrifice. It means we are reacting in a way that produces something beautiful. In that moment a gate is formed, a place of entrance where the King of glory can invade our situation.

Many people have no gate because they won't praise Him in the middle of apparent paradox. They get stuck wondering, "How can God promise to heal all of my diseases but I've got this problem in my body?" "How can God promise to provide, and yet I've been without a job for three months?" And yet Psalm 87:2 says, "The Lord loves the gates of Zion more than all the dwellings of Jacob." That gate—that place of praise in the midst of conflict—is where His presence rests, where the King Himself dwells. The gate is formed when we move above human explanation and into a place of trust.

People tend to respond in one of two ways when the answer they seek doesn't come. Let's see why those approaches don't work.

ACCUSING GOD...

When some Christians find themselves in a place of uncertainty with no answer for their problem, they change their view of God and ascribe to Him character traits that are totally anti-biblical. They might convince themselves that He won't help them out of a financial hole because He isn't intervening in their affairs, though the Bible says, "And my God shall supply all your need according to His riches in glory by Christ Jesus" (Phil. 4:19). They may claim He won't heal them, though the Bible says He heals all your diseases and forgives all your iniquities (see Ps. 103:3).

Uncertainty causes some people to misunderstand who God is. They begin to deny God's true nature and embrace sickness and disease, poverty and mental anguish as gifts from God. That is a devastating lie from hell. It's actually blasphemous to attribute to God the work of the devil. But many

THE *Supernatural* POWER OF A *Transformed* MIND

Christians want answers so badly during times of uncertainty that they invent theological answers to make themselves feel good about their present condition. In doing so, they sacrifice the truth about God on the altar of human reasoning. That's what causes people to say things like, "God gave my aunt leukemia to teach her perseverance." No way. That has never happened. If somebody's body is racked with pain or wasting away because of disease, it's the devourer. It's not the job description of the Messiah. Again, the Bible says, "He forgives all your iniquities; He heals all your diseases." It would never enter our minds that God would give someone a drug habit or a drinking problem to help them become better people. So why would He condemn people to disease? Or poverty? Or depression? Or any other miserable condition?

Let's get this straight: God is good all of the time. The devil is bad all of the time. We do ourselves a tremendous service to remember the difference between the two. Healing, salvation, wholeness, provision, and joy have already been given to us. They can't be recalled or returned. They are facts of Kingdom living. They were paid for by Jesus on the Cross.

Other Christians fall into the deception that when the Bible talks about sufferings, it means all of the above afflictions. Not at all! The suffering referred to in the Bible means living between two conflicting realities and trusting and praising God through it all.[1] Anybody can declare the greatness of God after they've won the Reader's Digest sweepstakes. But when you live in the middle of a conflict—of having a promise that is not yet fulfilled, or having a problem that seems to never get resolved—you rise above circumstance and declare that He is good all the time, no matter what.

Ramping Up Our Warfare...

Why do disease and addiction and all the other tools of the devil continue to torment the human race? It's my conviction that if we knew more about spiritual warfare, we could thwart much of what we see. What's needed to cure the incurable and do the impossible is warfare at a level that we have never experienced. There are two situations in the New Testament that support this view. In one, Jesus laid hands on a blind man and asked him if he saw anything. The man said, "I see men like trees, walking" (Mark 8:24). To get the complete miracle, the man needed a second touch from Jesus. He needed persistence. In another situation, a tormented child had a demon that threw him into the water and the fire to kill him. The father brought the boy to Jesus and said,

> If You can do anything, take pity on us and help us (Mark 9:22, NIV).

Jesus replied,

> "If you can"? Everything is possible for him who believes (Mark 9:23, NIV).

In other words, Jesus has no limitations and He is absolutely good all of the time. There was no question what He wanted in that situation, or what He could do. The responsibility for the impossible was not on Jesus but on the father of that child, and on the disciples who had been unable to drive out the demon.

Once while I was ministering in Southern California a mother brought me a child who was tormented by devils. The child scratched and clawed at me while I prayed and bound and did what I knew to do—and yet my prayers had no apparent effect. The mother looked at me and said words I will never forget: "Isn't there anyone here who can help me?" Why did that mother bring that child to me? Because I represented someone—Jesus—who is absolutely perfect, knows no lack of power, and is absolutely willing to bring deliverance. Is it reasonable to conclude that because I tried and didn't bring deliverance to the child that it was God's will for the child to be tormented? No, not any more than when the disciples tried but failed to bring deliverance. But that is the theology many people embrace during times of uncertainty.

Jesus said something completely different: "This kind can come out by nothing but prayer and fasting" (Mark 9:29). Jesus neither prayed nor fasted in that particular moment when He healed the demonized boy. But He had a prayer vault filled with time He'd spent with the Father so that heaven could erupt into the natural world at a moment's notice. He exercised faith out of intimacy with God, as we should do. My inability to bring the needed deliverance to the child has driven me to the throne. I must have more!!

When we find ourselves in uncertain seasons of life, we are like the disciples in that moment of failure. They were the most miracle-experienced people on earth at that time. No one had seen more and done more than they, and yet they came up against something for which they could get no solution. This is still true today. We may find ourselves facing problems and not knowing where the tools are to bring about the solution. But that doesn't mean the problem is insurmountable. There is power in resolving in your heart that God is good all of the time, and that His will for healing and wholeness does not change, despite what we see in the natural.

You can rest knowing that two things are guaranteed to you. First, in every situation in which you suffer loss by the devourer, all things will work together for good. Did God design the evil in your life? No. Did He assign it to you? No. But He is so big that He can win with any hand. He can use your past sin or the devil's attacks to accomplish what He wants.

Second, our God is a God of vengeance. The devil never has final say in anything. That beast will be silenced and there will be absolute, complete vindication for every moment of infirmity, affliction, difficulty, torment, and temptation that you've ever experienced. We have a promise from Romans 8:18 that says, "For I consider that the sufferings of this present time are not worthy to be compared with the glory which shall be revealed in us." The difficulty you experience in your finances, in that assault on your body, in that attack on your family or your emotions, is not worthy of comparison to the glory that will be revealed in you. Like Bob Mumford said a long time ago, "I read the last chapter and we win."

THE OFFENDED MIND...

The second thing that happens when some Christians face uncertainty is they often become intellectually offended with God. Mark 6:1-6 illustrates this:

> Then He went out from there and came to His own country, and His disciples followed Him. And when the Sabbath had come, He began to teach in the synagogue. And many hearing Him were astonished, saying, "Where did this Man get these things? And what wisdom is this which is given to Him, that such mighty works are performed by His hands! Is this not the carpenter, the Son of Mary, and brother of James, Joses, Judas, and Simon? And are not His sisters here with us?" So they were offended at Him. But Jesus said to them, "A prophet is not without honor except in his own country, among his own relatives, and in his own house." Now He could do no mighty work there, except that He laid His hands on a few sick people and healed them. And He marveled because of their unbelief. Then He went about the villages in a circuit, teaching.

This passage shows how an unregenerate mind is a horrible weapon that can be used against us, causing us to reject the very answer we need. The folks in Nazareth were stunned by Jesus' teaching at first. It stirred them up and caught their attention. When He started teaching in the synagogue, they said to each other, "Wow! Where did He learn this stuff? This is amazing!" They were impressed, and that created an environment in which Jesus could do miracles to illustrate the power of what He was teaching. But then they took stock of what was happening and said, "Wait a minute. We know this guy. He grew up here. We knew His dad, His mom, His sisters. How is He doing all these miracles?" Their minds became offended at Jesus. This is not the kind of offense where somebody hurts you. This is intellectual offense, when you have unanswered questions that block your ability to trust in the unseen.

Many times I hear people say things like, "I wish I could believe God heals people today, but my grandmother died two weeks ago and we prayed for her and she didn't get healed." Or, "I wish I could believe that God loves me, but I just went through a horrible divorce, and I know a good God wouldn't allow that kind of pain." Heartfelt, genuine grief separates people from God because they have questions, but no answers.

Questions are allowed in the Kingdom, but *lack of answers must not interrupt our heart-communion with God.* If we demand answers from God, then we are walking in the spirit of offense. Hosea 6:3 says, "So, let's press on to know the Lord." Those words "press on" can be translated "hunt." That's a picture of how we should passionately pursue the Lord, in spite of not fully understanding Him or His ways. We are to run after Him even in the time of potential offense. The answer is always on the other side of our offense. The Bible promised that, "We must through many tribulations enter the kingdom of God" (Acts 14:22). Getting through the difficulty—without becoming defiant or demanding with God—will take us into the very thing God promised.

David gave a good example to us when he commanded his emotions and his mind to come into line with the truth about God. He wrote in Psalm 103:1-2:

Bless the Lord, O my soul;
And all that is within me, bless His holy name!
Bless the Lord, O my soul,
And forget not all His benefits.

It sounds to me like he wrote that at a time when he was tempted to be offended with God. That's a terrific prayer for you and me to pray when we're in the uncertain place, ready to take offense with God. We can yank our minds and emotions back into line with reality.

When you find yourself in an uncertain time—and you surely will at some point—remember that you can create a gate of praise by lifting your heart and your voice to God. Persistently pursue fellowship with God even though your uncertainty feels deep and endless, and no answers have materialized. The suffering will last but a moment in God's grand plan for your life. Be thankful for the opportunity to persevere. And be assured—better times are on the way!

ENDNOTE

1. Biblical suffering is usually persecution for living righteously.

CHAPTER 9

LEARNING FROM YOUR BODY

*The human body was designed to live
in the glory of God...made to recognize God.*

My wife Beni and I were worshiping one Sunday morning at our church when a woman came forward and began to worship in front of us. It's busy up in the front of our sanctuary anyway, with flaggers and dancers, so I didn't think this was unusual. But then she started to do things that struck me as strange. When I say "strange," you have to understand, I have a pretty high tolerance for what might be considered odd behavior in worship. People have literally turned cartwheels in front of me in their worship before God, and it didn't bother me a bit. Some have worn war paint and camouflage to church, and one woman wore a wedding dress with combat boots as a prophetic declaration about the Kingdom. That's normal church for us. But this particular woman's movements didn't seem to flow from the Holy Spirit, and so I tried to discern what was happening in my spirit man—the location of the indicator that tells you something isn't right. Usually that gift works well for me, but this time it was as though the Lord reached into my heart and turned it off. I didn't feel anything, good or bad. I wasn't getting any spiritual signals about what was taking place before me.

But something unusual did happen: I noticed a shift in the temperature of the air around me. It got cold right where I was standing, probably 10 degrees colder than everywhere else. I remembered my brother, who is also a pastor, had encountered a demon in his office. His office was in a line of offices all on the same heating system. But after this encounter, his office stayed cold for an hour. People, not knowing what happened to him earlier, would walk in to his office and say, "Wow, it's freezing in here."

With that in mind, I investigated a little bit. I walked over to another part of the sanctuary and it was warm. I walked back to my seat and it was cold. I had a strong hunch that the devil was at work. I went to our main dancer and quietly asked her to worship before the Lord in dance on stage because we needed to break something in the spiritual realm. She got up there and began to dance and the moment she moved across the stage, the lady in front of me collapsed, as if she were a puppet and her strings had been snipped. Beni leaned forward and prayed with her. We discerned real sincerity, a heart that was right, but she needed deliverance and salvation. It turned into a wonderful story, but I want to draw your attention to the fact that signals in the physical realm—in this case, colder-than-normal air—helped lead to a spiritual breakthrough. The situation contained physical indicators of spiritual realities.

Present Your Bodies...

I mentioned briefly earlier in the book that the mind is grossly undervalued in charismatic/Pentecostal circles. The same is true of the physical body. Many see the body as evil in itself, something to be ignored, pushed aside, tolerated but never really used for Kingdom purposes. But God designed the human body to be more than a tent that you dwell in. It is

an instrument of God that recognizes His presence and dis-
cerns what is happening in the Kingdom realm. Romans 12:1-2
says,

> I beseech you therefore, brethren, by the mercies of God, that
> you present your bodies a living sacrifice, holy, acceptable to
> God, which is your reasonable service. And do not be con-
> formed to this world, but be transformed by the renewing of
> your mind, that you may prove what is that good and ac-
> ceptable and perfect will of God.

Christians use that passage mostly when sending off a
new missionary to a post somewhere overseas, or when people
do some other kind of ministry that involves self-denial. We
encourage people to offer their bodies as a living sacrifice by
volunteering at a Rescue Mission, or at a retirement home—
by going somewhere or doing something with their bodies.
I've heard people teach that when we raise our hands or
dance or kneel or lie prostrate in worship, we are offering our
bodies as a living sacrifice. All of those applications are true
and correct. But I'd like to suggest that this passage is also
speaking about our physical bodies' role in recognizing and
working with God. Let me develop this in the life of King
David, the man perhaps most acquainted with the presence
and the glory of God of anyone in all of history.

David had 30 to 40 years in which he came freely before
the actual, manifested presence of God that was upon the Ark
of the Covenant. God's glory radiated visibly from it. The
Bible makes it clear that David was immeasurably impacted by
God's presence. As a result he wrote,

> My flesh longs for You... (Psalm 63:1b).

Was he speaking purely metaphorically? I don't think so.
He was declaring that he'd been so affected by the presence
and the glory of God that his body itself ached and cried out

for more. What's true for David is true for us. In the same way that you and I might hunger for food or thirst for water, our physical bodies—not just our emotions, intellects, and spirits—can ache for God. And if we can hunger for God physically, then we can be satisfied by God physically. There is no such thing as hunger without the potential of fulfillment. You don't have an appetite for things that are non-existent. Rather, God has put within our makeup the capacity to recognize Him and His activities with our physical bodies.

Senses Trained...

Let's take it one step further. Hebrews 5:14 says a mark of maturity is having senses trained to discern good and evil. Touch, smell, sight, hearing, and taste can be trained to help us in the discernment process. Not only can we recognize the presence of God with our bodies, but those physical signs should help us discern good and evil. On that Sunday morning during worship, my spirit was telling me nothing about the woman in front of me, but the air temperature got the message across. Unfortunately, most Christians don't pay any attention at all to what happens to them physically when God shows up. They're focused solely on the intellectual or emotional side of things. They ignore one of the systems God gave us to perceive what's happening in the Kingdom realm. I've got news for you: God's first language is not English. He communicates with us in various ways, through impressions of the heart, mental pictures, feelings, emotions, and physical sensations. When we ignore our bodies, we are at least sometimes ignoring the voice of God.

This is important because when we neglect the physical signs of the Kingdom, we can miss what God is doing. Sometimes Jesus walks by our boat and does not intend to get in the boat, figuratively speaking. The Gospel of Mark says, "Then

He saw them straining at rowing, for the wind was against them. Now about the fourth watch of the night He came to them, walking on the sea, and would have passed them by" (Mark 6:48). He does that to let us know He is nearby, but the only way He'll get in the boat is if we request it strongly. He puts Himself within reach, but doesn't make it automatic. If we don't perceive that He is there, we will miss the opportunity. The disciples almost missed theirs because some thought He was a ghost. How much more do we misunderstand what we see and perceive physically with our senses, and miss opportunities to be with Jesus?

These days, I have seen many Christians open up to the ways God speaks. They are perceiving what He is doing, calling out for Him to come into the boat. They are stepping into the adventure that says, "I want every part of my being to be utilized by God, that I might be useful in every situation." One day it will be normal for all Christians to discern the Kingdom with their five senses. But to get there, we have to train our senses.

HOW DOES IT FEEL...

Pilots, when they're learning to fly, test themselves in flight simulators with the cabin pressurized as though they were at 40,000 feet. The instructor starts depleting the oxygen gradually so the pilot-in-training can recognize and observe what happens to his body when the airplane is losing oxygen. Every body responds differently. For some people, the hair on their arms hurts. For some, their ears ring. For some, the muscles in their legs ache. The important thing is to be familiar with how their own body reacts so if the oxygen masks don't fall properly, they can recognize from the physical signs that they are losing oxygen.

How do you react when God comes into the room in a special way? How do you manifest the presence of God? How do you feel, sense, or perceive God when He is moving around you? You need to know the answer to those questions to fully live the normal Christian life. Without understanding that God moves and communicates with us in the physical realm, our minds cannot fully come into line with heaven's reality.

For me, it's been a process of discovery. I learned that the tangible anointing, the presence of the Holy Spirit for giftedness, is physically discernable. I can physically feel it, as though someone took a silk scarf and laid it over my hands. Why is that important? Not so we can wow each other with what we feel. The point isn't competition. The point is fine-tuning our perceptive abilities so we know when God has come into the room, and what He intends to do.

I've spoken with people who get a tingling on the back of their heads, or a fire in their hands when God begins to move in a situation or place. I've observed in my own body that when somebody starts talking about revival or healing, my left hand gets hot. Why, I'm not sure, but the Bible teaches that the power of God is concealed and hidden in the hands (see Hab. 3:4). When somebody talks about revival or healing, they ignite the area of the affection of my heart and the anointing is released through those affections. Paul said, "You are not restricted by us, but you are restricted by your own affections" (2 Cor. 6:12).

One of our young men was walking through Safeway one time and he felt the anointing of God come on his hands. So he went around to everybody he could find in the store saying, "Do you need a miracle in your body? God is here." Everybody turned him down until he walked out of the store. A man was coming into the store. He asked him, "Do you need a miracle in your body?" The man said, "As a matter of fact I do. I'm in excruciating pain, and have had several back surgeries." He prayed for him and the man was instantly healed, then listened to the gospel and was born again. The young man began to shout in the parking lot that God had healed this man, and somebody else was saved. It all started with having senses trained to discern good and evil, and recognizing a "God moment" even in that unusual setting.

I'm not saying that we can physically feel every time God is at work. I am saying we should pay attention to the physical signs. You'll learn how your body reacts. It may take you years, like it has for me. Sometimes I'll pray for somebody and I don't sense anything, but they get healed. Physical senses are not always a sure indicator, but they are an indicator that God does use. Let's not stall on the adventure of learning to recognize God's presence. God will use every part of who we are. Tune into your body and begin to perceive the anointing and presence of God.

In the next chapter of this book we'll talk about one of the subjects dearest to my heart: dreaming and co-laboring with God.

CHAPTER 10

DREAMING WITH GOD

Absolute surrender to the will of God
is the only way for the believer to live.

Yet something strange happens as that person
enters into the intimacy of friendship with God;
God becomes interested in our desires. And ultimately,

He wants our minds renewed so that our will can be done.

By now I hope it's clear that the normal Christian life is a partnership between God and each one of us, played out in everyday living as we become the gate of heaven, releasing the manifestation of God's reality for those around us. Paul called us co-laborers with Christ (see 2 Cor. 6:1) and that is what we are—partners in the work of heaven in this earthly sphere. But many Christians have a one-dimensional perspective of this idea of co-laboring. They think it's a robotic interplay between themselves and God in which their will is dialed down to zero and His will completely overtakes their desires and thoughts. They see themselves as remote control beings, totally under the direction of a God who sits in heaven and works the master controls. But that is exactly the opposite of what the Bible says. In fact, our ideas and desires and dreams have a monumental influence on how God carries out His plan in this world. We are co-laborers, meaning that apart from Christ our work is not complete, and at the same time, amazingly, *His work on earth is not complete without us.* God looks to you and me as contributors to what He is doing, not just robots carrying out His ideas. He actually is interested in your desires and dreams and has opened up His plan on this planet to your influence.

This sounds almost blasphemous to the modern Christian ear. Many of us, myself included, have prayed prayers in the past that say, "Oh God, take over my will!" That is easily one of the stupidest prayers anyone can pray. It totally devalues our will, which is one of the greatest things God ever created. Your will is so valuable that He wouldn't violate it even at the cost of His own Son. You and I are the pearl of great price. Without an independent will, we become animated playthings, dolls, programmed toys. But with a free will, we become lovers of God and willing co-laborers with Him. And when we co-labor with Him, our ideas can literally change the course of history.

The Bible shows us how co-laboring works. At the creation, God let Adam name all of the animals (see Gen. 2:19). Names in those days were more than just cute labels given to distinguish the creatures. Names were assigned according to character. They indicated what kind of being this would be. When God gave Adam the privilege and responsibility of naming all of the animals, He was inviting him to assign character and nature to those creatures he would spend his life with. God created it all; Adam added his creative expression by giving the animals certain natures. That's co-laboring.

Another example is in the life of Moses. Moses had one of the most intimate relationships with God in all of Scripture. He experienced God face-to-face, even mouth-to-mouth, some say. How did that relationship work? One time God said to Moses:

Go, get down! For your people whom you brought out of the land of Egypt have corrupted themselves. They have turned aside quickly out of the way which I commanded them. They have made themselves a molded calf, and worshiped it and sacrificed to it, and said, "This is your god, O Israel, that brought you out of the land of Egypt!"...I have seen this people, and indeed it is a stiff-necked people! Now therefore, let Me alone, that My wrath may burn hot against them and I may consume them. And I will make of you a great nation (Exodus 32:7-10).

Moses responded,

Lord, why does Your wrath burn hot against Your people whom You have brought out of the land of Egypt with great power and with a mighty hand? Why should the Egyptians speak, and say, "He brought them out to harm them, to kill them in the mountains, and to consume them from the face of the earth"? Turn from Your fierce wrath, and relent from this harm to Your people. Remember Abraham, Isaac, and Israel, Your servants, to whom You swore by Your own self, and said to them, "I will multiply your descendants as the stars of heaven; and all this land that I have spoken of I give to your descendants, and they shall inherit it forever" (Exodus 32:11-13).

God's response?

So the Lord relented from the harm which He said He would do to His people (Exodus 32:14).

That's a breathtaking interaction. God wasn't playing some psychological game. He wasn't using reverse psychology to steer Moses to the right conclusion. He was interacting with Moses as a friend. This was a conversation between intimates, not servant and master. Jesus affirmed that we have this kind of relationship with God throughout John 14, 15, and 16:

No longer do I call you servants, for a servant does not know what his master is doing; but I have called you friends, for all things that I heard from My Father I have made known to you (John 15:15).

If you ask anything in My name, I will do it (John 14:14).

If you abide in Me, and My words abide in you, you will ask what you desire, and it shall be done for you (John 15:7).

Servants aren't co-laborers; friends are. There are major differences between the mentality of each. A servant is task-oriented, wanting to know exactly what is required so he or she can do it. But a servant doesn't know the master's business from the inside. We don't have servants today, so it's hard for us to understand, but imagine that you did have people living in your household who served you and carried out your will. A servant would know certain things about you, like your hobbies, whether you liked going to baseball games or out fishing, what you liked for dinner, what time you wanted coffee in the morning. But a servant would not share personal times with you. He wouldn't comfort you in your down times; you wouldn't invite the servants in to discuss family problems or major business decisions, or even minor ones. But God has elevated us from servants to friends. He invites us into a relationship that goes beyond employer-employee interactions. He is willing for us to engage Him...to change His mind, to direct His ideas, to share in His unfolding creative work. He doesn't lack for ideas. He just enjoys our participation.

When you become a friend of God, you don't lose the humility and obedience of a servant, but your relational perspective shifts. There is a point in our relationship with God where obedience is no longer the primary issue. That may also sound blasphemous, but it's a deep truth God wants to reveal more widely in the Church. There are levels of relationship with God that many of us have not conceived or experienced, and until we do, our co-laboring with Him will be more limited than it needs to be.

DAVID'S DREAM...

One of the most extraordinary examples of co-laboring was King David's idea for a temple. First Kings 8 recounts the building of the temple of Solomon, one of the most significant events in the Bible. At the temple's dedication, Solomon said,

> *Blessed be the Lord God of Israel, who spoke with His mouth to my father David, and with His hand has fulfilled it, saying, "Since the day that I brought My people Israel out of Egypt, I have chosen no city from any tribe of Israel in which to build a house, that My name might be there; but I chose David to be over My people Israel." Now it was in the heart of my father David to build a temple for the name of the Lord God of Israel* (1 Kings 8:15-17).

God said, "I didn't choose a city, I chose a man, and the temple was in the heart of the man." It's like He was saying, "The Temple wasn't my idea. *David* was my idea." Incredible! David's creativity and desires wrote history because God embraced them. This is absolutely foreign to most of our way of thinking. We wait for instructions and work hard to suppress our own ideas. We think anything we do for God must flow directly from the Throne and be carried out to the letter, as if from a heavenly instruction booklet.[1] God's approach is different. He has made Himself vulnerable to the desires of His people. History unfolds according to what we do, what we pray, what we don't do and what we don't pray. He gave us Kingdom principles that set up our parameters. Then He said,

"Dreamers! Come! Let's dream together and write the story of human history."

DESIRE...

Sometimes we think that if we really desire something, it must not be of God. It's as if we serve a barbaric God who wants to wipe out anything that springs from our own hearts. On the contrary, God is enamored of your desires. He wants to see what makes you tick. Yes, He made you and knows everything about you, but He can only commune with you as you open yourself up in relationship with Him. That's where pleasure is derived, when dreams and desires spark dialogue and interaction, and the co-laboring begins.

For many years I misunderstood the biblical concept of desire. Psalm 37:4 tells each of us:

> *Delight yourself also in the Lord, and He shall give you the desires of your heart.*

Like many pastors, I foolishly taught that if you delighted yourself in the Lord, He would change your desires by telling you what to desire. But that's not at all what this means. That verse literally means that God wants to be impacted by what you think and dream. God is after your desires. He's after intimacy with you. He has opened Himself to the desires of His people. He likes going back and forth with you, throwing out His idea and waiting for your response. Jesus even said, "Whoever you forgive, I forgive." Co-laboring is a huge aspect of ministry that many of us simply do not understand, because true friendship with God is so foreign to us.

Most of the misunderstanding comes because we don't know which of our desires come from God, and which are carnal. The very word *desire*² is made up of the prefix *de* meaning "of," and *sire* meaning "the Father." Desire is, by nature, of the Father. But before we come to Christ, our desires are corrupted because desire springs from what we commune with. If we commune with greed, our desires will be greedy. If we commune with pornography, our desires will be for perversity. If we commune with anger over a past hurt, our desire will be for revenge.

But when we commune with the Father, our desires are pure. Remember that Jesus said,

Whatever things you ask when you pray, believe that you receive them, and you will have them (Mark 11:24).

What do you desire when you are praying? What do you desire in that place of communion with the Lord? Once we come into the Kingdom, the straight and narrow road Jesus talked about becomes broad and big. The Kingdom is bigger on the inside than it appears on the outside. There is room for our desires, our creativity, our ideas. We don't think or dream independent of God, but *because* of Him. He essentially said, "I'm going to give you one huge idea, and I want it to shape every breath of your life, every bit of ministry, every prayer. The idea is, 'On earth as it is in heaven.' Now, go! Run with it. Make it happen."

That mandate moves us out of robotic servanthood where we constantly ask, "Lord, should I eat tuna or peanut butter for lunch? Do you want me to answer the phone when it rings? Should I talk to that person at the store, or pass by?" That's a form of dependence that doesn't always please God. Rather, God trusts the heart of a man who is lost in friendship with Him. As we come into intimacy with Him, more of what takes place is a result of our desires, not only of our receiving specific commands from heaven. God begins to feed off your wishes and desires, as He fed off of David's desire. The temple doesn't even appear to be God's idea, but it was so good that

He put it in His book and made it a big part of His work on the planet. *He will do the same thing with our ideas and desires!*

Likewise, the Bible says Jesus only did what He saw His Father do (see John 5:19). For most of my life I took that to mean that when Jesus put mud on the blind man's eyes, for example, it was because He saw the Father do it first in the spirit. I still believe that, but I also think Jesus was saying much more. I think He was telling us, "I see what moves the Father, and I allow what moves Him to set My course."

As a pastor, I know what it's like to watch other people's dreams flourish under the umbrella of the ministry at my church. But my first concern is always with God's agenda for us. When we consider other people for our board or leadership team, their agendas must go out the window. I don't pay attention to anybody's agenda, no matter how lofty it is or how much money they have to accomplish it. I am immune to other people's agendas until they lay them down and pick up my agenda, which God has given to me for our church. Then and only then, their agendas become important to me. Their desires and wishes come alive in my mind as they share them with me. I believe that's how the Father works. As He sees you and me surrender to His agenda, He's suddenly interested in hearing what we have to say. Our yieldedness and surrender make Him vulnerable to our dreams. It becomes a co-laboring effort.

As with any collaborative effort, the work we do with God bears our imprint and His. My wife gave birth to three of our children, and they bear my traits and hers. So when we co-labor with God, the result "looks" like Him and like us. For example, each of the four Gospels represents the same message, and yet each is unique and distinct, because each of the authors were unique and distinct. Even the present outpourings and revivals taking place across the world have completely different manifestations but the same Spirit because they flow through people with different giftings, personalities, relationships, and cultural settings.

Co-laboring isn't about having our way with God. He's not a cosmic bellhop to carry out whatever wish and desire we have. Neither does He rubber stamp every dream we come up with. But if He cancels one, it's only because He's got a better one in mind. And He would much rather listen to you dream than have you cower before Him asking for your next task.

ABOUNDING CREATIVITY...

Dreaming with God unlocks deep reservoirs of creativity in each and every person, in different areas of gifting and talent. But in too many sectors of the Church, creativity is on lockdown because people fear their desires and dreams. Religion, cruel and boring, bottles up the creative impulse God has put inside of every person. Each of us has a right and responsibility to express ourselves creatively in whatever area of life interests us. Yet so many of us have the horrible habit of doing things the way they have always been done, for reasons of fear and safety. We're descendants of the Creator and yet we stick with old, tired methods. We ask God to do a new thing through us, but expect Him to do it in a familiar way.

Many Christians pray, and when their mind wanders they think it's the devil distracting them. That may sometimes be the case, but maybe our "devil" is too active our God too inactive. When your mind wanders, maybe God is leading you to creative solutions to problems. You may have been resisting ideas from heaven and keeping to a rigid, religious practice of prayer. Some business people get "off track" when they're praying, thinking about a deal or an opportunity, and at the end of the prayer time they think, "I just blew my whole prayer time thinking about something else." Guilt and condemnation come on them when God was actually swerving them over to a subject that was on His mind. He wanted them to think creatively and to interact with Him so He could release ideas they'd never had before.

My uncle David told me one time that a professor at a Christian college looked at his students and said, "How many of you want to be millionaires?" They all said, "I do." He said, "Go home tonight and pray, and tell me what your feelings are while you are praying." They came back the next day, and he said, "How many of you want to be millionaires?" One person raised his hand, and that person went on to be a successful businessman. The point was, in this relationship with the Lord, there's an exchange in His presence, and it shapes passions and dreams in us. Unfortunately, religion has programmed us to shut down anything that might be a personal desire, so we let the world around us do the dreaming, and we draft into their dream. Many Christians never feel the liberty to creatively express what God is saying and doing in them personally.

As a kid in school, I had a bad habit of daydreaming. It has carried over into adulthood. Recently while sharing a meal with some friends in a restaurant, I found myself thinking about the healing power of God sweeping through that place. It was a "grown up" daydream. The next day a prophet prophesied over me and called out certain things God had put in my heart. He said, "You find yourself daydreaming…" and he described the things I was daydreaming about. Then he said in the voice of the Lord, "You thought all this time this was you, but it's Me! It's Me! I was doing that; I was in the middle of that dream; I was the one stirring that up in you."

Daydreams can involve all kinds of new, creative ideas. God deposits novel thoughts and ways of expression that we've never had before. What is it like to have the God whose thoughts are as high as the heavens speaking into your thoughts? Has it ever happened in your life? I read once that every four-year-old is an artist. Then they go to school and are taught certain standards for art, so not every child remains an artist. I wouldn't say the system is always bad, but there is a drive to create in every person that is sometimes squelched.

When my oldest son was two or three years old, he found the crayons and he drew what looked like the skyline of New York City on the wall. Beni and I thought it was terrific. Of course we didn't want him to draw on the walls again, but when we had guests over to the house, we said, "Come look at what our son did. He drew New York City on the wall."

Later, when he was about 10 years old, he was complaining about English class. "Dad, where am I ever going to use this?" he said. I listened to him go on and on about how boring English was, and I finally said, "Maybe you ought to pay extra special attention in English class. You might be one of those guys God uses to write books and you're going to need to learn this stuff." He got a faraway look and suddenly English class took on a whole new importance to him.

WITTY INVENTIONS...

A man was walking down the road a long time ago before there was AC electricity. They had to have a transformer every few feet from the power source all the way to where the power was going. This man let his mind wander over the problem and within ten minutes, God downloaded into his brain the entire concept of AC electricity, which allows electricity to travel for hundreds of miles without so many transformers. That one idea lit up entire cities from coast to coast. His daydreams revolutionized the world.

That's what the Bible talks about in Philippians 4:19 when it says "according to His riches in glory by Christ Jesus." A Jewish rabbi was asked about that phrase and he said, "It means God, out of His realm of glory and dominion, will release to His people ideas, concepts, creative things, and witty inventions that will cause tremendous provision to come to them."

God does not look at the AIDS crisis and think, "There's one I never thought of. Too bad nobody will ever discover an answer to that problem." He does not fret about the ecology or famine or any other problem the world faces. But until Christians decide to co-labor with God in unheard-of creativity and off-the-map dreams, we won't change the society and the world. We can't rely on God to do everything. We can't demand that He come up with all the solutions; we must co-labor with Him. In my personal experience, the more I come into an intimate place with the Lord, the more He blesses the labor of my hands with creativity and new ideas. That is God's desire for every person.

Pay attention to Kingdom imaginations. I don't mean the thundering voice in the sky, but the fresh ideas that gallop through your head throughout the day. It's entirely possible that they are sent to you by God. Some business people walk by a vacant lot and "see" a building sitting there, but they don't realize God is talking to them, drawing them to think creatively. Some musicians get an original tune stuck in their head, but they don't develop it. If we pay attention, we will pick up God's ideas. You see, the Church won't transform cities through continuous revival meetings but by allowing Kingdom creativity and power to flow into communities.

What would it be like to have ideas that transform a poverty-stricken area into a thriving business center? Or eradicate a particular disease? Or totally transform people's minds through a movie, book, or music CD? Why do you think there has been such an assault on artists in the Church? Because the enemy wants to separate us from the creative force that thinks outside the box. Those ideas can change the world.

THE TREE OF LIFE...

Your desires, far from being evil, are intended to make you strong and healthy in all areas of life. The Bible calls the fulfillment of your desires a tree of life. Proverbs 13:12 says,

> *Hope deferred makes the heart sick,*
> *But when the desire comes, it is a tree of life.*

Proverbs 13:19 says,

> *A desire accomplished is sweet to the soul,*
> *But it is an abomination to fools to depart from evil.*

When your desires are fulfilled, they become a tree of life to you. The tree of life provides continuous emotional strength, financial strength, wisdom, a mind that's at ease. That is God's desire for you and for every believer. The tree of life is mentioned in three books of the Bible. First it's in Genesis, in the center of the Garden along with the tree of the knowledge of good and evil (see Gen. 2:9). When Adam and Eve partook of the tree of the forbidden fruit, an angel blocked the way to the tree of life. It wasn't punishment; the tree of life added an eternal aspect to whatever it touched. In other words, if sinful man had partaken of the tree of life, mankind would have been permanently locked into a sinful condition.

The tree of life is mentioned again in the Book of Revelation 22:2, with a great prophetic picture of believers partaking of its fruit. That moment lies in the future and so the tree of life in Revelation tells us what will be. But the tree of life is also found in Proverbs, as we just read. The tree of life in Proverbs tells us *what can happen right now*. We can partake of the fruit of this tree in our everyday lives at this present time. God has figuratively placed this tree within our reach, and every bite of its fruit releases in us strength and eternal courage, a sense of destiny and purpose. Where does that tree spring from? From the fulfillment of our individual, unique, God-given desires. Desire is part of God's system, His economy. He draws us into intimate friendship with Him, then responds to our desires and prayers, and answers them. When He does, it releases the courage of eternity into us.

When our desires go unfulfilled, our bodies and spirits suffer together. One of the causes of sickness and disease is disappointment that is never dealt with redemptively. People go through a disappointing circumstance and never get before God to have Him heal the hurts they pour out from their soul. The physical body inevitably reflects what's going on. I once ministered to woman with Crohn's disease; her colon had been dissolving for seven years. I asked her if she struggled with shame. She said she did, and I said, "Your body is sending you a message. Your colon is eating itself. The harshness you have toward yourself is making you sick, and your body is manifesting what you are doing to yourself emotionally." She repented for that sin and was instantly healed.

When a tree of life grows sturdy in our spirits, it bears wonderful fruit in all areas of life. The Bible talks about the fruit of the Spirit—love, joy, peace, patience, and so on. These are produced when we abide in Christ, when our desires are fulfilled as we are connected to Him, the Vine.

That fruit should increase as revival and revelation are passed down through the generations, as we'll see next.

ENDNOTES

1. This principle is NOT to cancel out the fact that God has very specific plans and ideas, that we have no chance of changing. It's to our benefit to leave those concrete issues alone. What are they? You can only learn through relationship.

2. While this is not the etymological breakdown of the word, it does convey the principle represented by the word.

CHAPTER 11

INHERITING THE SUPERNATURAL

We have inherited every spiritual blessing in Christ.
He wants us to discover the "spending power" of our inheritance!

It's the Lord's desire that the supernatural territory we occupy, the realms of life where we consistently demonstrate His authority, grow larger and more powerful as we pass it on to the next generation. Inheritance is a biblical concept. Proverbs says,

Houses and riches are an inheritance from fathers.

Deuteronomy 29:29 says,

The secret things belong to the Lord our God, but those things which are revealed belong to us and to our children forever, that we may do all the words of this law.

What is the purpose of a natural inheritance? To give children a leg up so they don't have to start where their parents started. So they don't have to save for ten years to buy a house or start a business. Those who are blessed enough to leave something significant to their children give them a head start, with the hope that they will go farther, faster during their lifetimes. It's simply not true that everyone has to start at the same point and go through the same hardships. It's a biblical concept that one generation would provide a boost for the next.

A spiritual inheritance works the same way. It enables the next generation to start where the previous generation left off. It's the intent of the Lord for us to wake up to this, one of the most significant yet overlooked principles in the Christian life. He wants generations to pass on their spiritual inheritances. You see, with an inheritance, we get for free what someone else paid for. Sometimes we inherit graces from the Lord where we don't have to go through some of the processes a previous generation went through. That doesn't fit the do-it-yourself motto of the age, but it's the way it works with God. It's like when a person lays hands on other people to impart a grace for a certain area of life and ministry. Those people get the grace for free. That's the way things work in the Kingdom. We see somebody that has a great anointing in healing and we ask them to pray for us, and from that point on, we begin to pray for people and we see things happen that we never saw happen before. That's an inheritance.

A spiritual inheritance is about making us more effective and efficient in our representation of the King and His Kingdom. It is not for our gratification. It's delightful, it's enjoyable, it's pleasant, it's encouraging, but it's not simply for personal consumption. It is to open doors so that the King and His Kingdom have influence in more places than before.

A spiritual inheritance differs from a natural inheritance in one key way: A natural inheritance gives us something we did not have before. But a spiritual inheritance pulls back the curtain and reveals what we already have permission to possess. That's why it says, *but those things which are revealed belong to us and to our children forever.*[1] What's needed is simply the awareness of what is already there. Receiving a spiritual inheritance is like learning that years ago somebody put ten million dollars in your bank account. You had the money all along, but now you are at liberty to spend it, because you have knowledge that the money is there and belongs to you. This is what Paul was trying to get across when he wrote,

> *Therefore let no one boast in men. For all things are yours: whether Paul or Apollos or Cephas, or the world or life or death, or things present or things to come—all are yours. And you are Christ's, and Christ is God's* (1 Corinthians 3:21-23).

> *He who did not spare His own Son, but delivered Him up for us all, how shall He not with Him also freely give us all things?* (Romans 8:32)

> *But as it is written:*
> *"Eye has not seen, nor ear heard,*
> *Nor have entered into the heart of man*
> *The things which God has prepared for those who love Him."*

> *But God has revealed them to us through His Spirit.... Now we have received, not the spirit of the world, but the Spirit who is from God, that we might know the things that have been freely given to us by God* (1 Corinthians 2:9-10, 12).

When we learn of our inheritance, suddenly we have "spending power" with God. We call on resources we didn't know about before. When a previous generation passes on a spiritual inheritance, they pass on all the knowledge and experience they gained in a certain spiritual area.

TRAGEDY OF THE AGES...

But through 2,000 years of revival history, no generation has ever passed its revival to the next generation effectively. No generation has raised up the next to carry the momentum of a great outpouring of the Spirit, and then has had them take it to the next level. Time and again the ball gets dropped. The spiritual territory that was once occupied becomes unoccupied, and the enemy comes to repossess familiar turf. After some time another generation rises up, having become discontent, and begin to re-dig the wells of revival. But they start at about the same place as before. The well got filled with earth, symbolizing humanity, which is made of earth. We suffer setback after setback from generation to generation and what should be a point of passing the baton becomes a place of starting over.

The last 2,000 years of history show us that a revival will come and last two to four years, then fade out. Because of this pattern, an entire branch of theology has developed that says revival is supposed to arrive periodically to give the Church a shot in the arm—new enthusiasm, new hunger, new energy. But by saying that revival is an exception, a pit stop for refueling, normal Christianity is defined way down. I say rather that revival is not the exception; revival is normal. Signs, wonders, and miracles are as normal to the gospel as it is normal for you to get up in the morning and breathe. Revival *is* the Christian life; you can't dissect the two. We were never intended to live a season of life outside of the outpouring of the Spirit of God. He always takes us "from glory to glory" (2 Cor. 3:18). He is progressive in every move He makes. The nature of His Kingdom is that "of the increase of His government and peace there will be no end" (Isa. 9:7).

The tragedy of history is that revival comes and goes, and subsequent generations build monuments around the achievements of the previous generation, but do not completely receive and occupy their inherited spiritual territory. Perhaps they don't want to pay the same price their forefathers paid, or perhaps they end up forming organizations around past movements to preserve and defend the idea but not the practice of revival. In either case, they inherit territory for free, but do not pay the price to develop it, and so they lose it. You see, it's possible to live in inherited territory for a time without advancing that territory. But if we want to hold onto that territory, we must expand it, and to expand it we will have to pay a price.

The quickest way to lose something is to take a defensive posture where we maintain what we have instead of working to increase it. We learn that in the parable of the talents, where God condemned the man who did not put his money to use, but buried it in the ground. (See Matthew 25.) To choose not to expand and increase is to choose to lose the very thing we are trying to protect.

This principle is further illustrated in Luke 11:24-26 where Jesus said,

> *When an unclean spirit goes out of a man, he goes through dry places, seeking rest; and finding none, he says, "I will return to my house from which I came." And when he comes, he finds it swept and put in order. Then he goes and takes with him seven other spirits more wicked than himself, and they enter and dwell there; and the last state of that man is worse than the first.*

When a person gets set free, there is a moment when he is absolutely clean and purged from filthiness. From that moment on he has the responsibility of managing that liberty. Jesus used a house to illustrate it. The house is clean and swept, there's no furniture, no inhabitants there, but it's newly renovated and beautiful. It's now the owner's responsibility to set up housekeeping, to set up the furniture, to dwell in it, to occupy that home. One of our greatest problems is the failure to occupy the inheritance that we've been given.

Throughout the years, certain individuals broke into new spiritual territory: Smith Wigglesworth, Aimee Semple McPherson, A.B. Simpson, and many other giants of the faith we could name. They didn't start out as giants but they were possessed by a passion to pursue new territories that had not been occupied before, even when all logic and reason warred against them. They were like people on a safari chopping down undergrowth in the jungle to move into uninhabited territory. They were fed up with seeing one standard in the Bible and another standard in their experience. That discontentment caused them to move dangerously into territory that had been inhabited by violent beasts, if you will.[2] And so they began to possess territory that had not been possessed by anyone continuously since the days of the apostles. They did it at great personal risk and sacrifice, and entered into things that were completely unknown to the Church at that time.

But what was gained by past generations has not been occupied and advanced by those who followed. The house is swept and clean, but because it was not occupied, the enemy came back seven times worse. The word *house* in Scripture can refer to an individual, a family, a local church, a denomination, even to your ministry, gift, and calling. But our country is pockmarked by institutions that once were advancing into unoccupied spiritual territory, and then became re-occupied by the enemy. For example, one of these former hot spots from a few centuries ago was once a great revival center. For a season it became almost the focal point of the nation. If you wanted to see what God wanted to do on the planet, you could look there. That place was Yale University. Yale's goal back then was not to raise up nice Christian people, but to raise up Holy Ghost revivalists. They paid a price to move into uninhabited territory. But today the school isn't producing revivalists, but anti-Christian secularists.

How do you get from revival center to secular stronghold? Gradually, by one generation after another, yielding territory instead of embracing their inheritance. Compromise starts when we fail to maintain what we have been given, when we stop moving into new territory, from glory to glory. When they began to compromise in that vital area, they backed up. The territory they once occupied became inhabited by the enemy and the very thing that was once a strength now became their greatest weakness.

Show me a church or a family whose forefathers broke into significant signs and wonders in the realm of healing, and I can assure you that if the following generations did not work to maintain and expand that previous standard, they were heavily afflicted and diseased. When the victories of past generations go unoccupied, they become the platform from which the enemy mocks the victories of the past generation. Worse yet, that unoccupied territory becomes the military encampment from which the enemy launches an assault against the people of God to erase from their memories their inherited victories. When we back off of the standard that God has set, we literally invite the devourer to destroy.

Instead of building on the work of the John Lakes, Smith Wigglesworths, and Aimee Semple McPhersons, we build memorials to their memories, and forget what we should have inherited. We applaud the buildings they were in, we tell the stories of their great accomplishments, and the place that they occupied is now inhabited by the enemy himself. And so a generation like ours becomes dissatisfied once again, discontent at seeing a biblical standard and a lifestyle that falls short. And we once again have to re-dig a well, remove the humanistic, rationalistic approach to life that denies the Creator Himself and His involvement, intimate, personal involvement, in the affairs of man. We get back to the springs of life and joy.

A few hundred years ago a great revivalist named John Wesley began to occupy new spiritual territory. But first he came to the U.S. to be a pastor and had very little success. He boarded a ship to return to England, and he was depressed. During the journey they faced some terrible storms and he feared for his life, but there was a group of radical believers on board called the Moravians. He watched them and realized, "We don't know the same Jesus." He was already a pastor, but as a result of the presence and power of God on the Moravians, he was truly born again. He went back to England and became the father of the Methodist movement, a group of revivalists and fire-breathing believers. Thousands and thousands would gather in fields to hear Wesley preach. Having meetings outside was totally against convention, but Wesley and George Whitfield broke all the standards of the day. People would climb trees to see Wesley and he would warn them, "Don't get up in the trees," because the power of God would come and bodies would fall to the ground. God would sweep through those meetings. The Methodists had a slogan: "Organized to beat the devil." They were called "Method-ists" because they created structure, not for structure's sake, but to set the boundaries for God to do something significant in their midst. Their discipling process is legendary. They pastored 100,000 people through this process of raising up leaders who would raise up leaders who would raise up leaders. It's an amazing story.

And yet, within recent days, that very movement ordained a lesbian minister. Let's not misunderstand—Jesus loves lesbians, but He intends to get them out of that lifestyle. The point is, territory broken into by John and Charles Wesley, by John's wife, by those in leadership and the many forgotten revivalist preachers, has been lost. Through a lifestyle of risk, they broke into uncharted territory, riding horses from town to town to preach the gospel. Wesley put a stake down and passed that ground on to the following generation, and they built monuments to his accomplishments as they withdrew from territory he once occupied, trying to make the gospel more palatable, more understandable. After all, it's not necessary to suffer all that persecution, to have all those bad things said about you. They withdrew, perhaps out of good, reasonable intent, but they left vacated territory behind them, and the very things they were strongest in—great deliverance and freedom from bondage—have become their greatest weakness.

There are many other examples through history, but the point is simple. Every generation of revivalists has been fatherless as it pertains to the move of the Spirit. Every generation has had to learn from scratch how to recognize the Presence, how to move with Him, how to pay a price. The answer to this tragedy is inheritance, where you and I receive something for free. What we do with it determines what happens in the following generations. God is serious about returning for a glorious Church. He's serious that nations should serve Him—not just a token representation from every tribe and tongue—but entire nations, entire people groups apprehended by God Himself.

Can you imagine what would happen if entire nations stepped into the gifts they have from God? Where the song of praise, the declarations of God and His greatness and goodness became visibly manifest on a people? That's His heart. But if we're to get there, we must understand and embrace our spiritual inheritance. We were never intended to start over from scratch every two or three generations. God wants to put each generation at a higher level than the previous one. Every generation has a ceiling experience that becomes the next generation's floor. We dishonor our forefathers and the great price they paid to get their breakthrough by not maintaining and expanding what they accomplished. They attained by tremendous risk and persevering under ridicule and rejection. The things we take for granted today cost the previous generation tremendously.

DEFYING THE NATURAL ORDER...

Inheritance helps us to build truth on top of truth. Instead of starting over each generation, we inherit certain truths that allow us to move forward into new areas. For example, when we come to Christ, we become *servants* of the Most High God. Servanthood is a very strong reality of our relationship with the Lord. But there is a superior truth, and that is friendship. Friendship is greater than servanthood. Both are true, and we don't leave servanthood to become a friend, but we build friendship on top of the experience and revelation of servanthood.

That is how we are to move into new territory, by building on precept after precept. Truth is progressive and multidimensional. It constantly evolves as we grow, though it never evolves into something that contradicts its foundations. There are measures and levels of anointing that cause the reality of the Scripture to change for us. In fact, a generation is now forming, I pray and believe, that will walk in an anointing that has never been known by mankind before, including the disciples. This generation won't need natural illustrations to help them understand what their spiritual task is. They will move into spiritual territory that defies the natural order. I said earlier in the book that God wants to give us revelations and experiences of heaven that have no earthly parallel. Jesus told Nicodemus,

> If I have told you earthly things and you do not believe, how will you believe if I tell you heavenly things? (John 3:12)

Jesus had just used two natural illustrations to illustrate the Christian life. One was childbirth and the other was wind. Then He said He had more to say about spiritual realities that have no earthly parallel. This is important, because we are brokers of a heavenly realm. We are here as ambassadors assigned, given dominion over a planet, to represent His Name, to do what Jesus did. What good are we if we can't understand and operate in the spiritual realm that has no natural parallel? But as the generations embrace their inheritance, I believe we will move into the season Jesus spoke about that defies the natural order. Let me explain.

There are natural principles we live and work by in the things of the Spirit. We understand spiritual things through natural pictures. We compare evangelism to a harvest, because we are familiar with the process of plowing a field, making the dirt tender so it can receive seed, then planting, watering, tending, and harvesting. Those are the natural principles of harvest. But Jesus wants us to understand spiritual realities that have no natural picture. Jesus gave such a revelation that defies nature when He said,

Behold, I say to you, lift up your eyes and look at the fields, for they are already white for harvest! (John 4:35)

He meant that with a superior revelation not bounded by the natural order, every day is harvest day. There is no waiting for the right season. Those people who seem impossible to win to the Lord will be won instantly, without any sowing or preparation or tending, if our anointing is equal to the revelation Jesus has for us in John 4:35. The anointing on a coming generation will be great enough that the natural order of things will no longer apply. With a low-grade anointing and revelation, we have to live by natural principles and restrictions to get spiritual results. But Jesus brings this revelation, which is almost frightening. He says, "Lift up your eyes," meaning, "With the way you see things right now, you cannot operate on the revelation I want to give you. But there is something available for a coming generation where their anointing is so extreme that every person will be ready for harvest."

Jesus walked in such an anointing, carrying the Spirit without measure, which instantly defied the natural principles that illustrated spiritual truths. The more you and I become empowered and directed by the Spirit of God, the more our lives should defy the natural principles that release spiritual realities. It's not that the principles of harvest are no longer true. They are as true as they ever were, but they are superseded by a superior truth. What used to take years or months now takes weeks or days to solve.

Think of the Gadarene demoniac in Mark 5. The Church today would treat a man like that much differently than Jesus did. It wasn't long ago that Christians wouldn't even pray for an insane or deranged person. We sent them to asylums and to doctors to have their problem fixed. Now we at least have the courage to pray for them, and we're seeing break-throughs. Multiple personality disorders and people who have suffered satanic ritual abuse are made right with prayer, and what used to be beyond our realm of faith now can be broken with the anointing we have. But I still doubt if we would do what Jesus did: He sent the man into ministry right after being saved! We would probably insist that he go through a longer process of healing and deliverance before being entrusted the position of being the director of evangelism for that region. With the average anointing we carry as a people, we would have to take him through months of counseling sessions, and many training classes to make sure he is *debugged*. But as the anointing increases, it increasingly defies natural laws. You will know it is increasing because it will bump up against the very boundaries and limits of faith you used to live within.

Another example is this: Jesus came up to the fig tree, which had no fruit on it. It was not the right season for fruit. But He cursed it anyway. Why? Because He has the right to expect impossible fruit. He requires from us fruit that is impossible to bear. I said before, it is not normal for a Christian to not have an appetite for the impossible. It's completely abnormal; it's a deformity that comes through disappointment and/or bad teaching.

Remember the promise out of Amos 9:13,

"Behold, the days are coming," says the Lord,
"When the plowman shall overtake the reaper,
And the treader of grapes him who sows seed;
The mountains shall drip with sweet wine,
And all the hills shall flow with it."

That illustrates this very principle. We must lift our eyes to see from His perspective. A greater vision/revelation makes a greater anointing available, if I'll *earnestly pursue spiritual gifts*.[3] How do we know you've lifted them high enough? Because we can see differently—everyone ready for harvest. How does the plowman overtake the reaper? The growth stages are no longer restricted by natural laws of planting and harvesting, but have become supernatural in nature. The field is growing at the same time it is being harvested and planted. The seasons are overlapping. Why? Because a generation embraced its spiritual inheritance and in that new territory the anointing is strong enough to defy natural boundaries the Church has lived within for centuries.

FOLLOW THE GENERALS...

We are in the beginning stages of the season called *accelerated growth*. I believe it is possible under the mercy and grace of God to make up for several hundred years of failure in these areas. It is possible, if we are willing to pour ourselves out, to lay the groundwork for another generation to come and use our ceiling as their floor, to build upon it, to bring things of the Church into a place where it must come to.

Proverbs 13:22 says, "*A good man leaves an inheritance for his children's children.*" Righteousness causes us to realize that our daily decisions affect several generations away. We must learn to sow into the welfare of a generation we may never live to see.

I think of my father, who was a great general in the army of God. What I and my church are experiencing right now is beyond what I used to dream. But much of it, if not all of it, is because my dad paid a price. I watched him when I was a young man. I watched him push ahead as a forerunner, enduring so much criticism and rejection. He honorably displayed what it looked like to value the presence of God above the opinions and support of man. It cost him severely, but he left a rich inheritance for our family, as well as for the Church in our region.

In the final five days of his life, 20 or more family members were with my dad, singing praise and ministering to God, because that's what he taught us. He taught us that in all situations you give honor to God. It's our highest honor to bless His great Name and take delight in Him. He showed us how. So we were with him hour after hour, worshiping, giving glory to God, praying, sharing testimonies, telling family stories, finding time to rest in shifts, and then singing once again. We did this 24 hours a day in a constant cycle. And then he died. And we wept. We did all the things grieving families do. We were so sorry for our loss, happy for his reward.

Then I said to all the family members who were there, "Dad carried a mantle that can't be left here. An entire family must embrace it. We have an obligation to build on his ceiling, not to defend and protect what he accomplished, but to take it to' its natural conclusion and to walk in realms of dominion that have been made possible because of his sacrifice." Every individual, from the youngest to the oldest, surrounded the bed before we let anyone take him away and we prayed, "Lord, we receive that mantle of grace that is on this household because of the price this man paid."

I don't care if you're a first-generation believer, or if your family has been in the church for generations. By revelation you have access to an inheritance that is beyond your wildest imagination, beyond your wildest dream. We owe it to the generations in the past to occupy that territory because they paid a great price to bring it to us. We owe it to our parents, our grandparents, and to our great-grandparents. We owe it to our children, and their children. Before Jesus returns there will be the community of the redeemed walking under the influence of their inheritance, *a city whose builder and maker is God.*[4] There will be a generation that steps into the cumulative revelation of the whole gospel. There will be a generation that lifts their eyes and sees that supernatural season in which every single person is harvestable now, and have the anointing necessary to carry it out.

My cry is to see these things in my lifetime, so I'm giving my life for it. But I have told my kids and the young people I pastor, "If we don't get there together, take it on. Do not be shaped by the opinions of man, but be shaped by your value for His presence. *Any price you pay in claiming more territory for God is well worth the exchange.*"

ENDNOTES

1. Deuteronomy 29:29.
2. Exodus 23:29.

3. 1 Corinthians 14:1.
4. Hebrews 11:10.

For More Information

Bill Johnson
Bethel Church
933 College View Drive
Redding, CA 96003

Website: www.iBethel.org

Healing Our Neglected Birthright

DISC 1: *THE BATTLE FOR HEALING*
Any area of a person's life that is not under the influence of *hope* is under the influence of a lie, and *hope* is the atmosphere that faith grows in. As we consider Jesus' concern—when I return, will I find faith on the earth?—we realize that the battle for active faith, which results in an expression of authentic gospel, is His priority.

DISC 2: *IT'S IN THE ATONEMENT*
Sickness is to my body what sin is to my soul. The price that Jesus paid for my sins was more than sufficient for my diseases. Discover the full provision of the Cross.

DISC 3: *AUTHORITY AND POWER FOR HEALING*
Without power the gospel is not good news. Destroying the works of the devil was Jesus' mission, and is one we inherited at our conversion. To complete the task successfully, He gave us both authority and power. Learning how to function in these will enable us to increase our success in bringing people to salvation—from sin, sickness, and torment.

DISC 4: *PROSPERITY OF SOUL*
The mind and emotions of a person are not overlooked by the Gospel. The truth sets us free—spirit, soul (mind, will, and emotions), and body. The condition of the soul has a direct effect on our health. Some people receive physical healing by taking care of the "inner man."

DISC 5: *HOW SICKNESS COMES TO THE BELIEVER*
There are three principles that radically affect the health of the human body. When these issues are ignored we become *much* more vulnerable to affliction. Maintaining divine order in these areas pays great dividends for the whole man. Learn how to steward the principles that result in divine health.

DISC 6: *IMPARTATION*
It is natural for a Christian to hunger to see the impossibilities of man bow at the name of Jesus…and is unnatural to do otherwise. We are a people born to confront and reverse the works of the devil. It was written into our spiritual DNA. The fivefold ministry of Ephesians 4 is to equip the saints to do the work of service, which includes signs and wonders. this message is to bring every believer into a place to receive a greater anointing for healing.

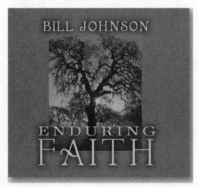

Enduring Faith

DISC 1: *ENDURING FAITH*
There is a rare faith that pleases the heart of the Father above all others—it's called enduring faith. It can only be developed in the tension of having a promise from God, yet living in its lack of fulfillment. In this place of extraordinary privilege, we have the chance to offer a sacrifice of praise and not lower the standard of God's promises to our level of experience. This moving message was given the week before the death of Bill's father.

DISC 2: *HOW TO HANDLE LOSS*
Many make it past the temptation to "curse God and die" after loss and disappointment—but not as many know how to keep themselves from the discouragement that leads to the sin of unbelief. This stirring message was Bill's challenge to his own church family after losing their corporate battle for his dad's healing. His father died only two days before this word was given.

These and many other titles available **@www.billjohnsonministries.com**, and **www.ibethel.org** or by phoning (530) 246-6000.

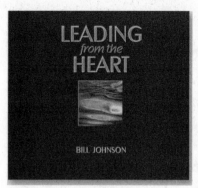

Leading From The Heart

What God is doing in the hearts of young and old alike is radically different from what we have seen before. But it's not new. God has raised up true leaders in the same way for centuries…with training that begins with the heart. Skills can be learned, but a Christlike heart comes through repentance, discipline, and encounters with God Himself.

DISC 1 & 2: *THE BACK DOOR TO THE THRONE ROOM*
People usually go to Bible schools receive training for ministry. Seldom do we realize that God's classroom is when and where we least expect it. And from His classroom we go through the back door to our promotion, if one is deserved. Facing rejection is an important feature in God's school. It will come to everyone who aspires to positions of leadership. Our faithfulness in this test determines how much authority we can be trusted with.

DISC 3: *LOYALTY AND RESPECT*
Proverbs 20:6 says, "Many a man proclaims his own loyalty, but who can find a trustworthy man?" God is saying that everyone thinks they are loyal, but He can't find real loyalty. Apparently, His understanding and ours are very different regarding this subject. The example given by God's generals in Scripture is very sobering. As leaders, we must learn this lesson with other leaders, or we will be sowing a crop we won't want to harvest.

DISC 4: *COUNTERFEIT AUTHORITY*
The spirit of Jezebel will try to attach itself to every ministry in existence. It works through manipulation and control, and exists in both men and women. The world's methods are often used in training spiritual leaders. The unintentional result is developing people who use manipulation and control to get others to co-operate with their righteous goals. The end does not justify the means. True authority comes through death. Competition and jealousy are signs that counterfeit authority is at work.

DISC 5: *DEVELOPING MINISTRY GIFTS*
There were at least five giant-killers in the Bible. Four of them followed the original giant-killer—David. Our relationship to those established in authority often determines the level of ministerial grace we are able to walk in. This message deals with the ways we receive life-changing grace.

DISC 6: *CHANGING THE WINESKIN*
Radical changes are in the wind. The church will look nothing like it does today in another ten years. The changes, although painful, are brought about by the Spirit of God. The wine that God desires to pour into His Church will break the systems that we function by today. The way we do church must change. The wine has been ordered, and is about to be served.

DISC 7: *DEVELOPING YOUR MINISTRY GIFT*
This message continues with the theme started in disc 5. God expects total devotion to the development of our gifts. Anything less is not worthy of Him.

DISC 8: *THE NEED FOR ENDURANCE*
This message was given in a Friday Night Renewal Service at Bethel Church, Redding, California. It was recommended that we add it to this series that's especially for leaders. This endurance message is a must for discovering God's purposes in our persistence.

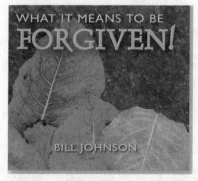

What It Means To Be Forgiven

DISC 1: *THE BOOK OF REMEMBRANCE*
Jesus bore the punishment that I deserve so that I might receive the blessing He deserved. His forgiveness is that complete! God remembers the details of your life differently than you might think. Once the blood of Jesus has touched our lives it redefines our histories. If we are going to be the people that help usher in the greatest move of all time, our self-concept must be consistent with His complete work at Calvary. Seeing Him as He is, and seeing ourselves through His eyes, are the keys to such transformation.

DISC 2: *GUILT FREE & LOVING IT*
The blood of Jesus destroys all our supposed "legal" rights to guilt and shame. To embrace either of these is to believe a lie. Flowing in the Holy Spirit is the great joy of the believer, and the guilt-free life is inherently more sensitive to Him. Learning to "move" with the Holy Spirit is the heart and soul of the Christian life.

These and many other titles available @**www.billjohnsonministries.com**, and **www.ibethel.org** or by phoning (530) 246-6000.

A CALL TO WAR

Kris Vallotton

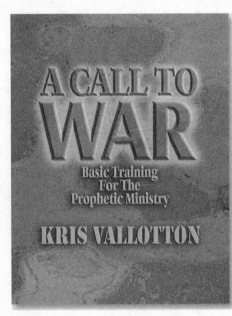

In a practical and easy-to-understand style, this manual presents the prophetic ministry in a way that "de-mystifies" the gift of prophecy and allows every believer to realize that God can and will speak through *you*!

A Call to War brings together the elements of reaching and practical application that will build a strong foundation for signs and wonders to follow.

Subjects include:

- Learning to Hear the Voice of God
- How the Gifts Grow in Our Lives
- The Purpose of Prophetic Ministry
- The Difference Between the Office of Prophet and the Gift of Prophecy
- Prophetic Etiquette
- False Prophets

Whether a pastor or leader wanting to develop prophetic ministry in your church, or an individual who simply wants to grow in this precious, life-changing gift of the Holy Spirit, *A Call to War* is a must-have tool that will bring life and wage war on the powers of darkness!

Kris Vallotton is the founder and overseer of the Bethel School of Supernatural Ministry in Redding, California. He is the senior associate pastor at Bethel Church and has been a part of Bill Johnson's apostolic team for over 25 years. Kris has trained and pastored prophetic teams all over the United States and is a recognized prophetic voice both here and abroad. He is a notable speaker with a vision and passion to equip an "Elijah generation" for the end-time harvest. Kris and his wife Kathy have been married for 29 years and together help to develop prophetic teams and supernatural schools all over the world. They have four children and seven grandchildren.

These and many other titles available @**www.billjohnsonministries.com**, and **www.ibethel.org** or by phoning (530) 246-6000.

Worthy of Support

If you want to sow into ministries that are bringing transformation to the cities and nations of the world, I recommend these two to you.

City Ministries International

Bob and Casey Johnson oversee a ministry that works in one of the darkest places of the United States—the streets of San Francisco. They serve the poor and broken of this world. This is a no-compromise ministry, preaching the gospel with both love and power.
www.City-Ministries.com

Iris Ministries

Rolland and Heidi Baker oversee a ministry that is bringing transformation to several nations in Africa. Thousands of churches have been planted in what will go down in history as one of the greatest movements of all time. The dead are raised, the blind see, and the poor are cared for. The gospel is preached with love and power.
www.irismin.org

Resources

The Bethel Church family of ministries has made a great number or resources available to help people enter into the greatest move of God in all history. The time is short. We must give ourselves completely to the privilege of shaping history through this great reformation.

Our materials range from refreshing worship CDs, a children's manual on the prophetic, and raising children with divine purpose. Go to:
www.iBethel.org

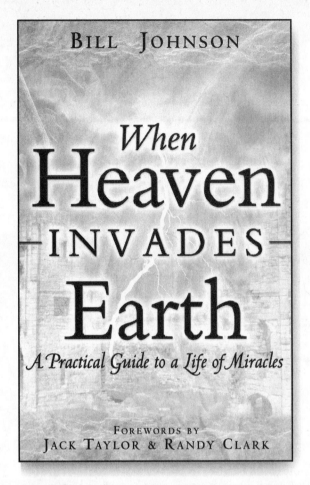

Additional copies of this book and other book titles from DESTINY IMAGE are available at your local bookstore.

For a complete list of our titles, visit us at www.destinyimage.com Send a request for a catalog to:

Destiny Image₀ Publishers, Inc.
P.O. Box 310
Shippensburg, PA 17257-0310

"Speaking to the Purposes of God for This Generation and for the Generations to Come"